Pearls
in
Arabian
Waters

"Boum" under sail. (Falcon).

Pearls in Arabian Waters

Peter Vine

THE HERITAGE OF BAHRAIN

© 1986 text: Peter Vine

© 1986 artwork: IMMEL Publishing

Phototypeset in Times Roman by
Lithoset Limited, Dublin.

Edited by Paula Casey.

Printed and bound in Japan by
Dai Nippon Printing Company, Tokyo.

Design and Illustration by
Jane Stark, Connemara Graphics, Ireland.

IMMEL Publishing,
Ely House,
37 Dover Street,
London W1X 3RB.

British Library Cataloguing in Publication Data

Vine, Peter
Pearls in Arabian waters: the heritage of
Bahrain.
1. Bahrain — History
I. Title
953'.65 DS247.B25

ISBN 0-907151-28-0

To Triona, Sinéad and Megan

The contributions of the following individuals and agencies are gratefully acknowledged:

EDITING

Paula Casey

PHOTOGRAPHY

Dr. Mike Hill
Anthony Nelthorpe
B.G. Morris
Sudhir Pradhan
Anthony Preen
Dr. J.E. Randall
Peter Vine
Walter Vreeland

Aluminium Bahrain
Bahrain Arts Society
Bahrain Environmental Protection Secretariat
Bahrain Telecommunications Company
Ballast Nedam
Department of Tourism and Antiquities
Directorate of Cultural Heritage
Falcon Foto
MEPA (Saudi Arabia)

ILLUSTRATIVE MATERIAL

State of Bahrain, Ministry of Information

STATISTICS

Central Statistics Organisation
Ministry of Commerce and Agriculture

DESIGN AND ILLUSTRATION
Jane Stark

CONTENTS

The "Tree of Life" (Vine).

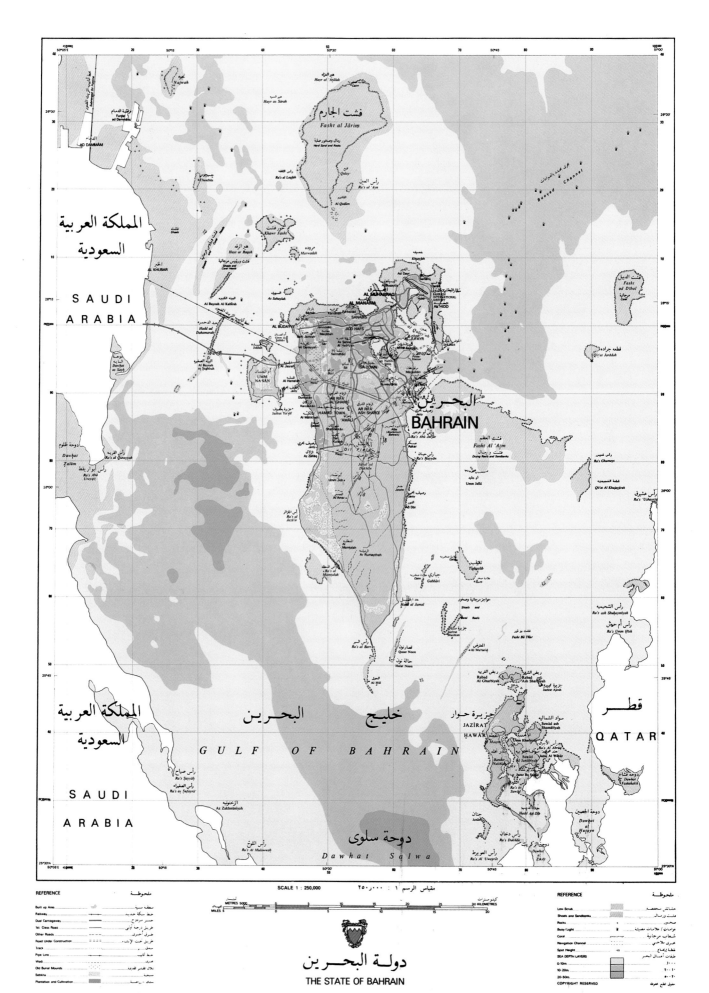

المملكة العربية السعودية

SAUDI ARABIA

المملكة العربية السعودية

SAUDI ARABIA

فشت الجارم
Fasht al Jārim

البحـرين
BAHRAIN

قطــر
QATAR

البحرين خليج
GULF OF BAHRAIN

دوحة سلوى
Dawhat Salwa

SCALE 1 : 250,000   مقياس الرسم ١ : ٢٥٠٠٠٠

دولـة البحـرين
THE STATE OF BAHRAIN

Printed at the Government Press, Ministry of Information - Bahrain

طبعت بالمطبعة الحكومية لوزارة الإعلام - البحرين

REFERENCE   ملحوظة

Built up Area
Railway
Dual Carriageways
1st Class Road
Other Roads
Road Under Construction
Track
Pipe Line
Wadi
Old Burial Mounds
Sabkha
Plantation and Cultivation

REFERENCE   ملحوظة

Low Scrub
Shoals and Sandbanks
Rocks
Buoy/Light
Coral
Navigation Channel
Spot Height
SEA DEPTH LAYERS
0-10m
10-20m
20-50m
COPYRIGHT RESERVED

(Photograph by Dr. Mike Hill).

Above, left: Tower of Portuguese Fort or Quala'at al-Bahrain. (Dept. Tourism & Antiquities).

Above, right: Gazelle have roamed across the plains of Bahrain since earliest time. They provided a challenging and rewarding quarry for stone-age hunters. (Vine).

Right: A hoard of silver tetradrachms provide evidence of Greek influence in Bahrain. (Dept. Tourism & Antiquities).

Opposite: Excavation of burial mounds has provided a wealth of information concerning the mode of existence of Dilmunites. (Vine).

THE PAST

It had been a long journey to reach the high ground. After the tidal sand flats and the lower plains this rocky terrain was harder going. On the final approach he had been surprised to encounter two streams and a pool of fresh-water springing out of the bare ground. In crossing the sand bar and a low, rain washed mud flat, he had noticed the tracks of several creatures he would like to hunt but there was no sign of any hunters foot-prints. He knew however that he must be careful for he had heard that a small tribe were living somewhere on this stretch of land. He was almost certainly hunting in their territory and had no wish to incur their anger. It was the first time he had ventured across the sand banks to reach this strange shore. His purpose now was to hunt for the "horned beasts" and small "grass-eating long-ears" that were both good to eat and provided useful skins. The cold wind had already started to blow and when the great sun slept they would need the skins to keep warm.

The ground he stood upon hardly qualified as a hill, let alone a mountain, but it was still the highest land for many miles and on this clear autumn morning he was rewarded with a panoramic view of the area. He wished he could have shared it with his fellows. As far as his sharp eyes could see low bushes were scattered over a plain where isolated patches of green vegetation told him water was to be found. Indeed, he could see the course of the two streams he had crossed and which he now realised flowed over part of the plain before disappearing underground, close to a low, steeply sloping cliff.

He was really a coastal dweller, more use to trapping fish and collecting shell-fish than stalking oryx, gazelle or hare. The journey was also much longer than his parents had ever had to travel in search of skins. . . Anyway, he reflected, the walk had been worthwhile. The trap set the previous night had caught a fine white "horned beast" he had skinned with the aid of a sharp stone brought with him. As he stretched the skin over the sun-baked rocks a feeling of security comforted him. With a little more luck he would return with three big skins and around twenty of the "grass-eating long-ears" together with enough meat to feed them through many sun-sets. After a while he gathered his stone tools, and went in search of food for his immediate needs.

Despite being alone, and somehow afraid of the fact that he was outside his own territory, he was quite happy. There was an atmosphere about this whole region which he liked. Perhaps he would bring the rest of his tribe here. There seemed to be more wildlife to hunt, there was adequate fresh-water, and the shallows between the "big-land" and this area had good stocks of fish. The only problem was the other tribe already living on the coast. Perhaps they would accept him. He pondered on this as he quickly made his way down the hillside towards the place where he had seen the hares playing. If his luck held he should be able to kill several with his spear.

Nine thousand years later, a small gathering of clothed gentlemen who spoke in a language few local people could understand, and one our hunter would

Jebel ad Dukhan is the highest point on Bahrain, rising to 122.4m above sea-level. (Vine).

This collection of (c.8,000 year old) Neolithic stone-age flint arrow heads tells its own story of early man's hunting activities on Bahrain. (Dept. Tourism & Antiquities).

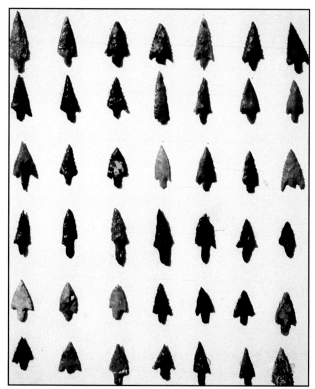

have found totally incomprehensible, were standing in exactly the same place on Bahrain's Jebel ad-Dukhan. They gazed across a semi-desert, dotted with sparse vegetation and, in contrast to those earlier times, they had no need to locate foot-prints as evidence of Man's presence. Tarmacadam roads criss-crossed the dry earth and on the southern slopes of the hill huge aerials of a tropospheric scatter station loomed over the landscape. At the foot of the Jebel was the site where Bahrain's first oil-well had been spudded in 1931.

These twentieth century gentlemen had not come to Jebel ad-Dukhan in search of food or clothing but they were looking for something. While one dug in the shallow mixture of gravel and rubble, another sifted the debris and carefully picked out fragments of stone. They had discovered the remnants of flint tools possibly left by our lone hunter. Their scientific report would provide firm evidence of how Man lived on Bahrain more than three thousand years before the island became the focus of the civilisation known as "Dilmun".

While it seems likely that Man had occupied the region for many thousand years before that time, it is perhaps not surprising that little evidence of his presence had been discovered for its inhabitants were, for the most part, coastal dwellers, and their sea-shore has since been covered by a rise in sea-level. Indeed from around 80,000 years ago to about 20,000 years ago much of the Arabian Gulf was dry land and the estuary of the river which flowed across it was situated further south, to the north-east of present day Oman. Then, gradually, as the great polar ice caps once more melted, sea-level rose until, at about the time when our hunter friend was at Jebel ad-Dukhan, Bahrain finally lost its land-bridge with the Arabian mainland. His Stone Age tribe were eking out their existence along the shores of what is today Eastern Saudi Arabia, trapping fish in the shallows, eating shell-fish and collecting wild fruits. While there have been no discoveries of settlements on Bahrain dating back as far as this period, a nearby site at Shagra on the mainland of Arabia has been dated to 5020 BC. It consists of the remains of a hut made from Tyrrhenian sandstone together with remnants of fish, shellfish, flint arrow heads, stone pestles and grooved stones.

In the same period their counterparts in today's Northern Iraq were entering a crucial phase of development which was to be the precursor of the great civilisation of Mesopotamia. Their cultural acceleration resulted from learning to domesticate animals and to grow crops. This success in creating dependable food supplies led in turn to an increase in population and the small settlements became villages eventually growing into cities. Thus, the cradle of early civilisation was established and Bahrain's proximity to it meant that the Mesopotamian influence was soon felt.

This book celebrates a new phase in the development of Bahrain. Seven thousand years after the land bridge with Arabia was severed, a new link has been constructed which once again allows Man to move from Arabia to Bahrain on dry-land! There is no doubt that this project will bring benefits to both Saudi Arabia and Bahrain and that the causeway will exert a considerable influence upon regional development. But, looking back in time, over the

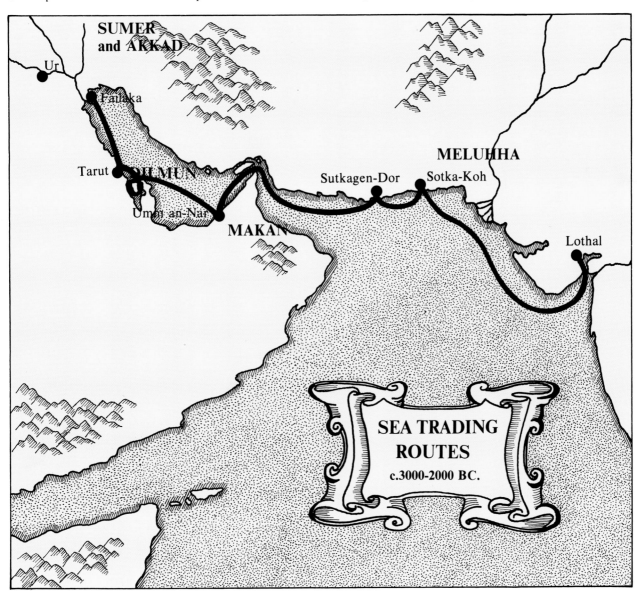

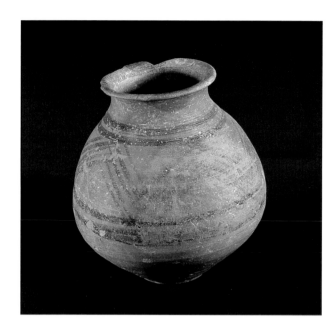

Early pottery jar around 2,800 to 2,300 BC. (Dept. Tourism & Antiquities).

thousands of years which have created Bahrain and its community, it is apparent that its aquatic isolation has been a positive factor in its growth. It led to the development of a discrete culture and forced upon its inhabitants the need to master the maritime skills of seamanship and navigation, not to mention boat design, boat building, diving, fishing, sail-making, and trading. From its earliest days, the geographic position of the newly created island of Bahrain placed it in a position of considerable importance for it was a natural staging post where fresh-water and other supplies could be replenished, on both north-south and east-west navigational routes.

Bahrain's first settled communities appear to have been established around 4,000 BC. Shell middens from that time have provided the clues demonstrating how these people depended upon the sea and were living in small family enclaves. Investigation of a midden dating back to the same period at Al Markh suggests that the site was occupied on a seasonal basis by fishermen who used it as a temporary base and a place for fish curing. Their earlier fishing was based upon shallow traps while later efforts progressed to the use of boats and capture of bigger fish or even dugongs. Concurrently the great civilisations of Sumeria were rapidly expanding and trading links were operating between Eastern Arabia, known at that time as Dilmun, and ancient Sumerian cities such as Uruk. Clay tablets excavated from Uruk mention such trade with Dilmun. Ubaid pottery found in the shell midden at Al Markh date contact between Mesopotamia and Bahrain as being established by 3,800 BC. These trade-links resulted in unique cultural influences bringing Bahrain in closer touch with the Dilmunite communities of the Arabian mainland. Unique, because in Dilmun the religious cults of Mesopotamia were absorbed and moulded by the strongly maritime Bahrain-Dilmunites into a singularly characteristic civilisation which was both independent from, and significantly different to, its mainland counterparts. Around 2,500 BC the ritual centre of Dilmun moved to Bahrain and, by 2,000 BC the civilisation of Dilmun was at its height.

We knew of Dilmun's existence as an ancient civilisation of major importance before we knew where it had been situated. Our earliest knowledge came from the translation of tablets extracted from the ruins of Mesopotamia's ancient cities. In 1880 an archaeologist and distinguished philologist by the name of Sir Henry Rawlinson wrote:—

"throughout the Assyrian tablets, from the earliest period to the latest, there is constant allusion to an island called Niduk-ki in Accadian and Tilvun or Tilmun in Assyrian, and that this name, which unquestionably applies to Bahrain. . ."

Despite Rawlinson's dogmatism this assertion had not, at that time, gained wide acceptance. Whereas the ancient civilisation of Egypt, Assyria and Babylon had been studied and excavated, this was not true of Dilmun. In the latter case we knew of the existence of an ancient civilisation as a result of interpreting the findings of these other sites, but nobody could say for sure where Dilmun had existed. The most recent records of it were about 2,500 years old! Since then it had simply disappeared from written history. By the end of the last century the search for this lost civilisation was beginning to gain momentum. Sir Henry Rawlinson's assertion that there was no doubt that Dilmun and Bahrain were one and the same place stimulated further research and investigations on the island eventually uncovering many of the secrets of the Dilmunites. The twentieth century has been a period of continued enlightment regarding Dilmun and, with that knowledge has emerged the history of Bahrain — an island which for thousands of years has traded on its unique position and its remarkable range of natural resources. In studying its history one is continually reminded of the unique facility which the inhabitants of Bahrain have demonstrated for analysing international conditions and reaching decisions on their own course of development taking best advantage of these external factors. Throughout history, Bahrainis have been proud to belong to Bahrain and have remained sensitive to its special cultural heritage. But we should not digress too far at this stage from the discovery of Dilmun.

The disappearance of the name Dilmun from the written record, about two and a half thousand years ago is all the more remarkable when it is realised that for two thousand years before this Dilmun had been a flourishing civilisation playing a key role in the trade and cultural development of the area. The Dilmunites themselves were sea-faring and travelling people who had ranged to distant lands as far away as Greece and to the borders of what is today Thailand.

Rawlinson's conclusion that Bahrain and Dilmun were one and the same place resulted from the work of an archaeologist and young British army officer: Captain E. C. Durrand who, in 1880 published the

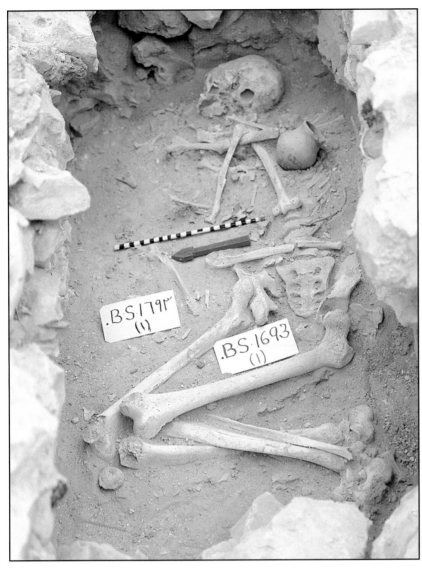

Left: Burial chamber and skeleton from a burial mound excavated at Hamad town (c.4,500 years old). (Dept. Tourism & Antiquities).

Below: Ancient burial mounds near Hamad town are monuments to Bahrain's early history. These date from the civilisation of Dilmun, around four thousand years ago. (Dept. Tourism & Antiquities).

A Barbar pot (2,500 - 2,300 BC.
(Dept. Tourism & Antiquities).

results of his survey of Bahrain's antiquities. The most prominent and compelling of these had been the ancient burial mounds which Captain Durrand was quick to observe:—

> "On nearing the coast, while dusty ground — the relic, probably of former habitations — intrudes everywhere; and mighty mounds of bare vegetation tower above the palm groves. Mass upon mass, mound upon mound, they stretch on in endless chains all around the slope that falls from the cliffs to the sea, clinging more particularly, perhaps, to the higher ground, but being found in separate clusters near the coast itself. . ."

At first he assumed that these were some form of ancient habitations but later, after observing the large mounds of Aali he wrote:-

> ". . . made me doubt the correctness of my first conjecture that they must be temples. Still, as they were the only distinctly shaped mounds of their size that I was able to examine closely, while immediately behind them stretched chain upon chain, and group upon group of lesser tumuli, unquestionably graves, I clung to the hope that this large group might be something more. But if these miles upon miles of crowded heaps are tombs, where did the inhabitants live? Probably they lived along the coast as at present, building their houses of the branches of the palm-trees, as do the poorer classes."

He went on to conjecture that the islands may have been a cemetery for the inhabitants of Gerrha which was situated on the adjacent Arabian coast. His fascination with the mounds led him to carry out several excavations confirming that they were all burial mounds. His account of entering one of the largest tumuli is worth recounting here:—

> "APRIL 6th 1879:— I can now give a further account of the larger mounds that I have since been engaged upon.
> "In the first place, I chose the most perfect looking of the large tumuli, the present height of which is about 45 feet, circumference 200 paces, and the circular mound around it 330 paces, 20 paces of level ground separating this latter from the base of the mound, with a line of wall joining the outer circle to the base of the mound.
> "I naturally thought that this mound might cover the ruins of a small circular temple, and not those of a tomb. So we began to work at the top and centre, cutting down several yards. Finding, however, nothing but a ring of large stones, I left the top and began work again a few feet above the base, running a cutting into the mound and taking care to retain the same line east and west, having remarked a depression or shallow channel from the

top to the bottom of the mound in this direction. Here, on going in a few feet, our progress was blocked by enormous stones, which appeared, on removal, to form part of a cyclopean circular containing wall. One of the blocks we had to break up with the crow-bar measured roughly over six feet long, by three feet six broad, and eighteen inches deep.
"The height of this wall above the ground level of my tunnel was about seven or eight feet, which would make it at least ten feet high from the level of the ground. The blocks used were unequal in size and unmortared.
"On breaking through this wall, I almost at once found myself in a passage or gallery, about six feet broad, and gradually narrowing (as I found afterwards) to five feet three inches at the inner end. The walls on either side were of rough unmortared, and carelessly fitted stones, varying in size, but sloping pyramidally upwards from the encircling wall and also slightly outwards from their base. I picked my way between these containing walls, removing the earth as I went, and thus gradually clearing out the passage behind as we proceeded.
"This increased the labour enormously, and was I believe unnecessary, from the compactness of the mass, the relative small size of our gallery, and the outward slope of the walls.
"A second barrier or inner wall, which blocked the entrance to the tomb itself was met with at a distance of thirty feet six inches from the first circular wall of blocks. On nearing this inner wall we found the passage on either side to be roughly mortared, and where the well-welded barrier forbade access, the wall on either side had two coats, one of rough and the other of smooth mortar, the latter underlying the former, which still here bore the marks of the plasterer's finger smears. The undercoat was of different material, and so smooth and hard that we had to use our picks to remove it. The transverse wall of cemented blocks had been built in apparently after the side-walls had been finished. We blew this out.

"From the platform on which these blocks were placed, a drop of three feet six inches brought us to the smooth and mortared floor of the tomb; here we turned up, among the stones and rubble masonry, a large amount of charcoal in such big pieces, that I think the roof must have been at one time supported by date tree trunks. Some pieces of a thinner character presented the appearance of bamboo-matting charcoaled.

"On the right and left of the passage were two shelves on either side, the lowest of which was carefully lined with mortar, but held nothing but yellow dust, with which they were filled up. These were four feet long, by eight inches in depth, and were at a height of six feet nine from the ground to the platform. There is nothing to show to what use these shelves have been put. On descending from the platform (the end of the passage) the walls carefully mortared still continued right and left for three feet two inches, and then turned at right angles, forming small mortuary chambers of the same shape as those in the lesser tomb previously described.

"The dimensions of these chambers right and left of the passage are roughly seven feet three (length), by three feet three (breadth), and five feet six (height). From the interior walls of these chambers stretched back, through piles of rubble and fallen blocks, the side walls of a passage some four feet broader than the gallery by which we had entered.

"To give an idea of the size of the stones used, there is a big mass now lying in the passage, probably a whole stone, and one of those that formed the roof, the dimensions of which are five feet long by four feet broad, and two feet nine in depth, and another lying alone in the left hand side chamber, five feet long by one foot ten thick. Of course, all round, over and under these, there are smaller masses buried in mortar, flints and earth. Though I searched most carefully, I found no marks of writing anywhere, not even a mason's mark on any of the stones."

Durand also sketched the large mounds at Aali and captured their real magnificence before their appearance was altered by further excavations, local interference, and by their conversion, in some cases,

into kilns. Throughout these excavations Durand had been searching for some sign explaining the origin of the tombs. He failed to find any writing on their walls but, convinced that any people who went to such trouble to bury their dead must have also developed communicating skills, he had carried out an earlier search resulting in a discovery, the importance of which Durand could hardly have guessed. He had started his hunt by visiting old mosques but having failed to locate anything of interest he paused for a while:

> "At last, having visited twenty mosques at least, which produced nothing but a cup of coffee, a kallian. . . I was told of a stone that nobody could read. This, therefore, I went to see, and found it embedded in the "holy of holies" in the Madrasseh-i-Daood, in the Bilad-i-Kadim. The stone is of black basalt shaped like the prow of a boat, or an animal's tongue, and is two feet two inches long."

He obtained the stone which was to produce a key unlocking the secret to the whereabouts of the ancient civilisation of Dilmun. It's 3,750 years old inscription reads as follows:—

> "Palace (of) Rimum, servant of (the god) Inzac, man (of the tribe of) Agarum"

Mention of the god Inzac alerted Rawlinson to the link between Dilmun and Bahrain. In earlier work translating tablets from Assyrian excavations he had discovered a tablet providing a list of gods with the regions under their protection. One of the lines had read:—

> "The god Enzac; the god Nabu of Dilmun"

Reference to Enzac on the Bahrain stone was enough for Rawlinson to stake his reputation on the Bahrain-Dilmun link. His treatise on the subject, published in Journal of the Royal Asiatic Society (New Series, XII (Part 2) 1880) provided a post-script and series of comments upon Captain Durand's discoveries which were published in the same volume, Rawlinson's paper is a masterpiece of linguistic interpretation, intellectual discussion and intuitive deduction. Although not all of his conclusions have proven to be correct it is remarkable how right he was on many points. In his book: "Dilmun Discovered", Michael Rice comments on Sir Henry Rawlinson's exceptional energy as follows:—

> "This was the enthusiasm demonstrated by Enki ordering the World, in one of those Sumerian myths of which Rawlinson was, as it were, one of the midwives; Enki has his place in Rawlinson's exegesis, as must be the case in anything dealing with the ancient Gulf. . ."

After Durand's work on the tombs of Bahrain, published in 1880, there was a gap of more than twenty-six years before another comparably thorough investigation was carried out, this time by Colonel F.B. Prideaux who was serving as 'political resident' of the island. His report was published in the Archaeological Survey of India (1908-1909). Prideaux's survey of the tombs centre especially on the larger mounds around Aali but also included some smaller ones. Between October 1906 and April 1907 he supervised the excavation of seven of the larger mounds and twenty-five smaller ones. His report is accompanied by some excellent photographs of the inside of various tombs showing their highly organised structures and some of the pottery and human remains which he discovered. In terms of answering the question of their origin however he drew a blank and, in his own words described the findings, after much effort, as "meagre".

Almost twenty years after Colonel Prideaux's study of the tombs another British archaeologist reopened the excavations. Ernest Mackay was despatched to the island on the instruction of Sir Flinders Petrie who had himself made an immense contribution to the study of ancient Egypt. Petrie had alluded briefly to the intriguing question concerning the origins of the great cultures of Pharaonic Egypt in one of his articles in the magazine "Ancient Egypt". With remarkable insight he had written:—

> "The strong Mesopotamian suggestions of the designs have, as we have noted before, no exact parallels in the East. They seem rather to belong to a people of Elamite or Tigrian origin and ideas, who had progressed on their own lines. The presence of shipping as an important factor would be against their having come to Egypt across the Arabian desert. The probability seems that they have branched off to some settlement in the Persian Gulf (such as the Bahreyn Islands) or on the South Arabian coast, and from their second home brought its style and ideas into Egypt".

It was clear that Petrie had good reason to suspect that there were greater archaeological remains to be found in Bahrain than had so far been discovered. In Mackay he had chosen a young but experienced archaeologist who had excavated in Palestine and India. In a precise and methodical investigation of the tumuli he opened thirty-four mounds and found human remains in twenty one of these. As with previous workers, he was disappointed in the relative paucity of remnants but he did unearth a number of bronze objects and one delicate but unfortunately damaged ivory figurine of a girl. One of Mackay's most significant contributions was the detailed drawings he made of the tombs (see fig. 1).

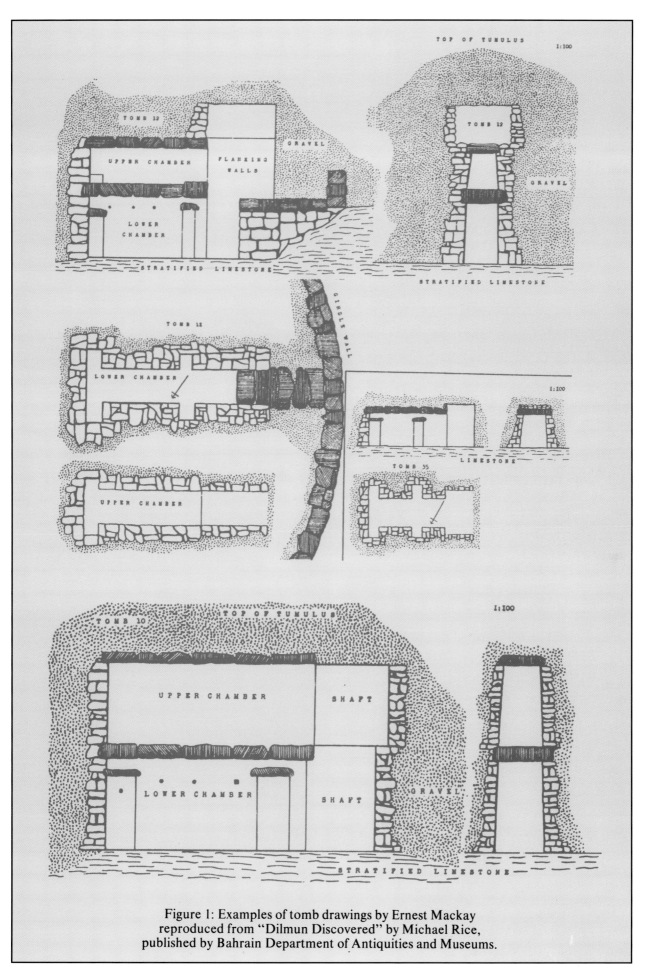

Figure 1: Examples of tomb drawings by Ernest Mackay
reproduced from "Dilmun Discovered" by Michael Rice,
published by Bahrain Department of Antiquities and Museums.

Right: Barbar temple during its excavation phase. (Dept. Tourism & Antiquities).

Below: Barbar jar. (Dept. Tourism & Antiquities).

Opposite: The south front of the Barbar temple clearly indicates the terrace walling of two periods. The section with the stairway is part of Temple II while to the right of that is the wall of Temple III, which later obscured Temple II. In the upper left of the picture is the central court of the temple. (Vine).

There are a number of reasons why the tumuli of Bahrain have yielded relatively little in the form of preserved remains, pottery, ornaments or implements of the Dilmunites. Firstly, the weather has played a major role in the destructive process. Bahrain experiences intermittent heavy rain which, over the centuries, has soaked through many of the tombs. In order to keep them dry the mounds were covered in limestone chips but this waterproofing allowed puddles to form around their bases and, in many cases, the water then flowed into the burial pits. Unlike the wonderfully preserved Pharaonic tombs in Egypt's Valley of the Kings, Bahrain's earlier graves were not tunnelled into solid rock and were thus left unprotected from water erosion. In addition, grave-robbers entered nearly all the mounds on the island — destroying or removing many of their preserved remains in the process. In such a situation it takes extra careful detective work by archaeologists to unravel the story behind a particular burial.

The tombs were more recently excavated by a number of archaeologists including a series of Danish expeditions commencing in 1953 and continuing somewhat sporadically until now. The excitement of their quest for Dilmun and the convincing evidence of their numerous excavations are well reported in Geoffrey Bibby's book: "Looking for Dilmun". In this account of the Danish group's work on the island, Professor Bibby recounts how depressed they were when they discovered that the first tomb they excavated had been largely destroyed by grave-robbers of some previous age. He relates how, as a result of painstaking work, his team were able to deduce the original position of the corpse, to confirm the presence of an ostrich egg drinking cup and to reconstruct a pottery vase from the many small sherds which they found buried in the sand, under a slab of stone pushed in by grave-robbers. Their inch by inch search even revealed two fine copper spear-heads lodged in a crevice under the roof slab.

At this stage the Danish archaeologists were not much wiser concerning the origin of the inhabitants who had built the grave-mounds covering vast tracks of the island. Despite efforts of previous excavators

there was still no evidence of the substantial dwellings which must have existed on the island if the grave-builders had also been resident there. Mackay had drawn attention to this point and had in fact proposed that the grave builders must have travelled from other areas in order to bury their dead on the island. Following his account of their first tumuli excavations, and the paucity of results therefrom, Bibby comments as follows:—

"Now this could mean that Mackay's theory was right, that the people who built the grave-mounds had not lived on Bahrain. Or it could mean that we had not looked in the right places. But we had, after all, covered the ground pretty carefully — and the settlements lived in by the builders of a hundred thousand grave-mounds ought to be fairly thick on the ground. . ."

The answer, as he was soon to discover, lay not on the ground, but under it. Whereas this might seem to be self evident the situation in Bahrain was somewhat unusual in that the grave-mounds had not been covered by accumulated soil and Stone Age flints lay on the surface of the ground just as they had been dropped many thousand years ago! Why therefore should anyone have thought that the major cities of this ancient race lay beneath ground level?

By a process of deduction the Danish team reached the conclusion that, since suitable settlement sites on Bahrain were mainly influenced by the proximity of fresh-water, and that the same factors had been at work for a very long time, it was most likely that the elusive ancient towns lay beneath existing settlements. The realisation led them to concentrate their efforts on locating "tells" (or city mounds) in the north of Bahrain, where fresh-water springs are found.

Their first major investigation of such a mound took place at Barbar where, instead of uncovering, as they had expected, an ancient village, they discovered that the mound of sand and gravel was in fact part of an ancient temple. Despite the fact that their excavation was far from complete they were quick to recognise the affinities of its layout with that of ancient temples of Mesopotamia. Bibby described the scene as follows:—

"It was not a temple of a type we had ever seen before, but there seemed no doubt about its nature. In the centre the circular structure was now revealed as an oblong platform framing two circles. Their purpose was still uncertain but they looked very much like plinths for twin statues. To one side of them stood an upright slab of stone and a foot or so away lay another, with the precise place where it had stood still marked in plaster on the stone paving. Both had hollows on the upper edge, and when the second stone was set up again it was obvious that they were supports of a short bench or stool. In front of them stood an altar, a cubical stone with a square hollow on the upper surface, and in front of that again stood a stone with a round hollow leading into an open stone drain sloping down to a hole in the surrounding wall. In front of this whole complex there was a square pit in the courtyard, framed by slabs of stone standing on edge."

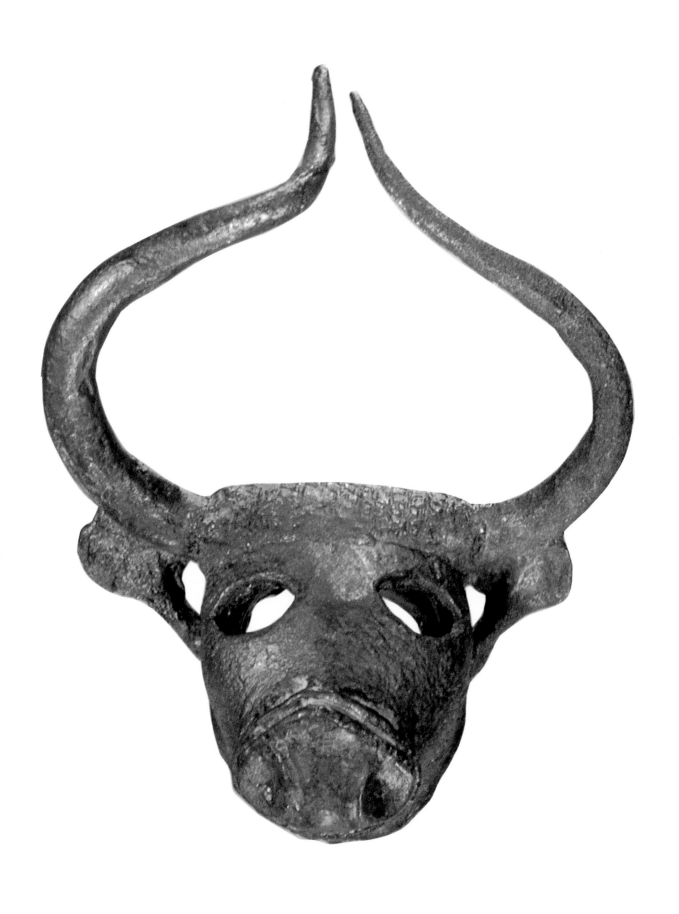

The Bull's head discovered in a corner of a room at the Temple II at Barbar. Lying alongside it were a heap of copper bands and sheet copper pierced with nails. Eyes of the bull were originally inlaid. The head stands 20cms high and was cast in the round. (Dept. Tourism & Antiquities).

It was an arrangement which immediately brought to mind the scene depicted on many Mesopotamian seals — i.e. a god seated on a bench with an altar in front of them and the worshippers offering their gifts. With this in mind the archaeologists immediately directed their attentions to the pit in front of the altar. Sure enough, they found there potsherd, lapis-lazuli beads, alabaster vases, a copper figure of a bird and a copper statuette of a naked man standing in exactly the pose of supplication depicted on ancient seals recovered from Mesopotamian ruins. This then was a temple to which villagers from this ancient civilisation had come to pray to their god for their needs. The statuettes were gifts left behind as a symbol to remind the god of their visit after they had left. Their early finds left the Danes in little doubt regarding the age of their discovery since the copper figure of the naked man was clearly Sumerian and could be dated to somewhere between 4,500 and 3,800 years old.

The discovery of the Barbar temple contributed enormously to our knowledge of Bahrain's ancient history. Since its unearthing in 1954 intensive study has shown that there are in fact four temples on the same site, constructed in five different stages. Three occur on top of each other while a fourth, known as the N.E. Temple, lies in a separate, smaller tell northeast of the main tell. The three overlying temples are as follows:—

TEMPLE 1.:— a Sumerian style temple consisting of a double stepped platform with the lower platform oval in shape and an upper square one. There were two wing structures, a basin and an enclosure. This temple was partially covered by Temple II so complete excavation is not possible.

TEMPLE II.:— was basically similar to Temple I but it has been better preserved since finely worked limestone blocks from the island of Jidda were used.

TEMPLE III.:— was different in form and was badly damaged. It was built on the levelled remains of Temple II but instead of having extension wings a separate temple — the NE Temple was constructed at the same time so that a double-temple was created.

The earliest temple has been linked to the late Akkadian period and four more building phases took place, with the latest occuring in the Old Babylonian period. Religious traditions of the earlier temples suggest similar links to those which influenced the Ninkurzag Temple at Al-Ubaid in Mesopotamia. This evidence implies that the gods were of importance to the cult of the Dilmonites — i.e. Enki, Ninkurzag and Inzac. The basins or pools of temples I and II were symbols of the second underground sea or "abzu" of which the god "Enki" was the ruler. There are other features of the temples which indicate that the cult worshipped a pair of gods and in this case the second deity is likely to have been Ninkurzag who, we know from Mesopotamia, was the consort goddess of Enki.

The fact that the third and fourth temples are built to a new plan suggest new developments in the cult's practice of worship.

While the Danes continued in their excavations of the Barbar temple a small team had commenced work on a "tell" adjacent to the "Portuguese Fort" also along the north coast of Bahrain. The site is more properly described as the Bahrain Fort or "Qal'at al Bahrain" since the Portuguese built their defensive ramparts on the site of an older fort. The low mound now recognised as a city mound measured about 600 yards from west to east and extended three hundred yards southward from the beach. Under it lay the remains of at least one major city.

Excavation of the city soon demonstrated a link in time between one level of this dig and the Temple at Barbar. There was still some doubt however, concerning the age of the gravemounds until a chance find provided a convincing connection between the mounds and the Barbar temple. Geoffrey Bibby reported on the event, involving a Bahrain based Church of England vicar called Alun:—

"... he had walked into camp one afternoon with a large cardboard box. They were making a new road up at Buri, he said, and it passed through one of the large mound fields above Aali. He had been driving along it today, and had seen that one of the bulldozers had cut away half a mound, exposing the central chamber. He had stopped and climbed out and pulled a stone or two away to break into the chamber. And there inside lay a pot, which he had brought with him in case we were interested, he opened his cardboard box and lifted out and placed on the table a typical ridged, red, egg shaped, short necked, triangular rimmed, 'Barbar culture' vessel. I remember that we gave him a beer..."

It is not difficult to imagine the excitement which the chance find generated. It was now clear that about four thousand three hundred years ago a substantial population of people lived in the city at Qal'at al Bahrain and that they built a temple to worship their gods Enki and Ninkurzag at Barbar, three miles to the west. Their dead were laid to rest in the tomb mounds which had first alerted archaeologists to the possible existence of an ancient Bahrain civilisation. The pottery found at Barbar and in the tomb was different from anything unearthed at other ancient excavations. Later examinations of Barbar pottery have shown that more than 95 percent of it is locally made (known as "Barbar-ware") but as one moves up the sequence from the earliest levels, there is a clear progression of techniques and development of characteristics as in, for example, "chain-ridged-ware". The distinctive nature of Barbar ceramics has led to the conclusion that this was a separate community and culture which, while it had

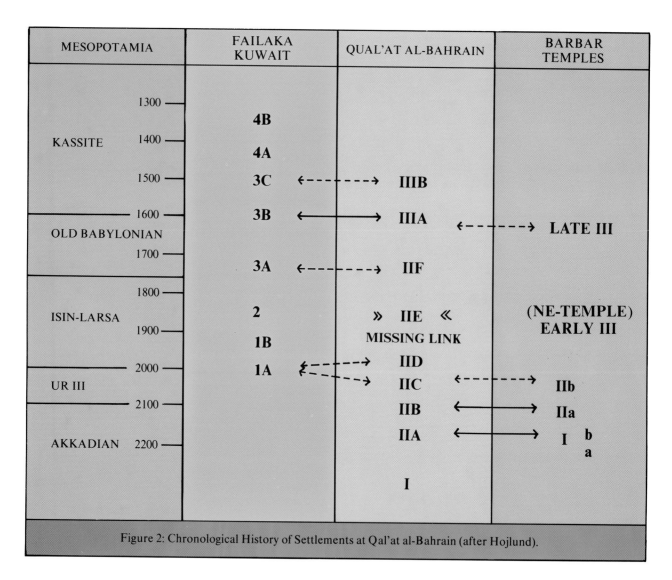

Figure 2: Chronological History of Settlements at Qal'at al-Bahrain (after Hojlund).

communications with Makan (Oman), Mesopotamia and Meluhha (Indus valley civilisations), it retained its own individuality.

Work by the Danish archaeologists and subsequent investigations have enabled us to draw a reasonably detailed chronological history outlining the various construction phases of the settlements at Qal'at al Bahrain (see fig. 2).

As a side issue to the main excavations the Danish archaeologists discovered an ancient shell-heap composed of pearl oyster shells. In the midst of the shell mound signs of hearths and fish remains were found — supposedly the scraps left behind by pearl divers. Associated with the hearths were scattered pieces of potsherd and when two pots were reconstructed they proved to be of the red ridged-ware type already discovered at the Barbar temple. Thus it was shown that pearl divers were among the Bahraini inhabitants who worshipped at the Barbar temple (about 4,300 years ago).

A further clue to the activities and affinities of this ancient culture was provided by the discovery of stone seals.

While the seals were indicators of the trading activity and maritime communications of Bahrain four thousand or so years ago, the real evidence of its commerce is to be found on clay tablets which were discovered, largely by chance, in the excavated house of a gentleman named Ea-nasir who had lived in the Mesopotamian city of Ur around 3,780 years ago (i.e. 1813 BC to 1790 BC). The find was made by Sir Leonard Wooley during a well planned excavation of Ur in 1930-1931. Fortunately for us, Wooley decided to carry out part of his exploration among the ordinary houses of the city instead of concentrating entirely upon the ancient temples and tombs. His discoveries were to prove of critical importance in elucidating the lives of these ancient people and in helping us to understand the part Bahrain (Dilmun) played in the nurturing of civilisation. Ea-nasir dealt in copper and the tablets found in his house recorded his business communications, not all of which were complimentary regarding his ethical standards. One message to him from a customer called Nanni was quite blunt in its criticism. It read as follows:—

"When you came, you said: "I will give good ingots to Gimil-Sin". That is what you said, but you have not done so; you offered bad ingots to my messenger saying: "Take it or leave it". Who am I that you should treat me so contemptuously? Are we not both gentlemen? . . . . . Who is there among the Dilmun traders who has acted against me in this way? . . . . "*

24   THE PAST

(* free translation by Geoffrey Bibby in 'Looking for Dilmun')

Other tablets provided lists of cargoes received from Dilmun. The main item was usually copper and one of the tablets makes it clear that this did not originate from Dilmun but was received from elsewhere. The Dilmun traders were acting as a clearing house for this and other goods. From the tablets we know that considerable quantities of copper were involved; in one case a shipment received at Dilmun weighed 18.5 metric tons! The copper originated in fact from 'Makan' which has been identified with Oman. The payment received in Dilmun was mainly in the form of wool, garments, skins and sesame oil.

It seems clear from recent discoveries that the Dilmunites were the first people known to us who practiced tooth extraction and the art of dentistry. This conclusion is based upon an examination of the dentition of the skulls removed from grave mounds dated to around 2,000 BC. It is even possible that some of the dentistry tools of the period have been discovered since two pointed objects unearthed by the Danish archaeological team bear an extremely close resemblance to modern dentists' elevators. Given their rich diet of dates, jam, beer, raisins and figs, it is hardly surprising that tooth decay and tooth ache was widespread among the early Bahrainis and that the art of tooth extraction was thus developed at an early stage.

Some of the fascinating discoveries concerning Bahrain's ancient history have been provided by Bahraini sponsored excavations under the aegis of the Department of Antiquities in the Ministry of Information. One such recent project was the Arab Expedition excavations at Sar el-Jisr led by Dr. Moawiyah M. Ibrahim from Yarmouk University in Jordan. It was the first detailed study of the Sar burial mounds and results of the Arab team's work are published in a report issued by the Ministry of Information in 1982. Subsequently the mounds were excavated by a Bahraini team of archaeologists directed by M. Rafique Mughal whose 540 page report was also published by the Ministry of Information in 1983. These excavations uncovered remarkably dense and extensive burial complexes together with many artefacts including Barbar pottery; Dilmun seals; Copper-bronze spearheads and knives together with numerous beads.

More recently excavations of burial mounds at Hamad town have uncovered additional evidence of how Dilmunites lived. Among a vast number of discoveries, one which has captured the interest of the general public is that of a four-thousand year-old gold and pearl ear-ring. The find has finally put to rest any doubts which archaeologists still held concerning the ancient significance of pearls. The sixteen member team of Bahraini archaeologists who made the find were led by Professor Corethia Qualls, an American Fullbright scholar.

In order to gain a clearer picture of Dilmun and its people I spoke to Professor Qualls shortly after she had completed her season's excavation work. Her comments reinforced the views of many archaeologists who have become increasingly impressed over the type of civilisation which existed in Dilmun. "It would be a terrible mistake to under-estimate the high living standards of its inhabitants" she told me. "While the mounds may not be as spectacular as the tombs of the ancient Egyptian pharaohs, the big difference in Dilmun seems to be that there was a great equality of high living standards among the inhabitants. Whereas in Egypt only the rulers and wealthy were buried, here everyone was placed in a tomb. We are gradually piecing together the story of their everyday lives. They had animal sacrifices; used bronze weapons; made fine pots; ate dates; kept goats, sheep and cows; fished for a variety of sea-foods and took considerable care over burying their dead."

Dilmun Seals.

(Hubert de Haas for State of Bahrain, Ministry of Information — from "Excavations of the Arab Expedition at Sár el-Jis", by Dr. Moawiyah Ibrahim, 1982).

Kassite period pot from City III at Qal'at al-Bahrain. Made from honey-brown clay the pots of this period (c.1,800 - 1,200 BC) are of quite a different shape to those from previous periods. (Dept. Tourism & Antiquities).

Among the shell-seals discovered during the excavations were forty-five new kinds and Professor Qualls believes that there is a case to be made for claiming that the world's first seals were made from shells and that Bahraini seals made from local shells were perhaps the fore-runners of the more elaborate seals which followed. Another clear factor to emerge from these excavations is the evidence of trade and movement of people throughout the region. Bronze weapons discovered during the work were made from copper originating in Oman while some pottery patterns suggest that they were brought from, or the designers were influenced by, civilisations in Baluchistan, Pakistan and India.

In this way, the story of Dilmun gradually unfolded as a result of archaeological detective work and a certain amount of luck. Research continues and each year some new evidence emerges which confirms earlier conclusions or else throws new light upon the lives of the Dilmunites. To those who visit Bahrain today, it is hard to imagine how an ancient civilisation could have existed there without the comforts and technological support of our modern society. It is true that a great part of the island is arid desert or semi-desert and the climate is at times uncomfortably hot. It must be remembered however that Bahrain had something which was far more valuable than copper or gold and was in extremely short supply throughout the region — namely clear fresh-water. There is no doubt that the island's role as a place where vessels

could provision themselves for long voyages was a major influence in extending the boundaries of exploration and trade. The fresh-water springs along the north coast of Bahrain provided the life-blood for the local population and for the crews of vessels sailing through the Gulf. Bahrain thus developed as an entrepôt and the island's wealth grew as a result of its trading and warehousing as well as locally based agriculture activities.

Dilmun's geographical position also played a major role in its development as a cultural and trading centre. Prevailing northerly winds make sailing up the Gulf a difficult task involving continued tacking and vigilance to prevent running aground on coral reefs or sand banks. Thus the vessels which crossed the Indian ocean, or skirted along the coast from Meluhha, were more than happy to find a location towards the south of the Gulf where they could off-load their goods and return, rather than prolong their voyage by beating up the Gulf of Mesopotamia. Vessels from Makan had a much shorter distance to sail but they too could, if they so wished, take advantage of Bahrain's position and shuttle their cargoes of copper between Makkan and Dilmun while other vessels were left to specialise in the northern passage.

Apart from the importance of its geographic position in terms of physical navigational considerations, Bahrain also held an important strategic position. Around 4,000 years ago, during the Old Babylonian period (2,017-1,712 BC.) Dilmun capitalised on its natural resources and its location to develop from a refuelling station to a merchant power capable of exercising a degree of control over vessels passing up the Gulf. As part of their network of look-out posts they built a base on the northern island of Failaka lying off the coast of present day Kuwait. Thus the boundaries and influence of Dilmun were extended in a clearly defined way, beyond the shores of Bahrain and its adjacent islands. The purpose of this controlling network was to force vessels sailing north or south to dock at Dilmun. This period marked the height of Dilmun's wealth and influence and then, almost overnight, records of Dilmun ceased.

One of the most recent accounts of it, which has been dated to 1,744 BC, referred to a shipment of copper from Dilmun. Despite the fact that its international importance declined, Dilmun continued to exist and to trade with Mesopotamia, Makkan and Meluhha. The Aryan invasion of Meluhha occuring in the middle of the second millenium BC seems to have put an end to trade links with Meluhha and thus caused a rapid decline in the wealth and importance of Dilmun. We know from clay tablets dated to the Kassite period (14th century BC) that Dilmun of that time was mainly exporting dates. The Kassites (who had invaded Mesopotamia in 1,750 BC) enjoyed an expansionary phase which resulted, for a period at least, in them exercising a degree of control over

A bowl made from Steatite or soapstone (c.770 BC). (Dept. Tourism & Antiquities).

Greek coins including the head of Alexander the Great. (Dept. Tourism & Antiquities).

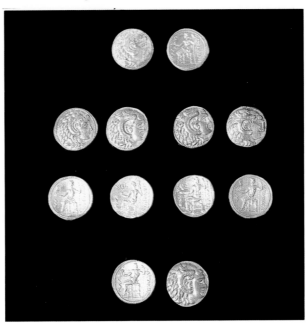

Bahrain. Their rule over Mesopotamia came to a halt in 1,200 BC when the Assyrians conquered that vast region and from around 750 BC the Assyrian kings claimed sovereignty over the islands. Soon after, trading links with India were re-established and Bahrain enjoyed a revival. In the late fifth century BC Dilmun was annexed as part of the Babylonian Kingdom but in 539 BC their influence over the island ceased as a result of an attack by the Achaemenid dynasty of Persia.

Despite the local upheavals which the various changes must have brought, Bahrain continued to play an important role as an offshore, strategically situated, maritime trading nation throughout the remainder of the first millenium BC. The Greeks knew of its existence in the 4th century BC and referred to it in their maps.

Alexander the Great sent three vessels on a reconnaissance mission to the Arabian Gulf in 325 BC. He had already conquered much of Asia and had rested for a while at what is today Karachi where he had ordered the construction of a fleet of ships. While he took the overland route back towards Babylon he instructed his Admiral Nearchos to explore the coast of Baluchistan and Persia before returning to

Left: A beautiful example of a Hellenistic flask (300BC - 200AD).
(Dept. Tourism & Antiquities).

*Below: An aerial view of Arad fort, built by Bahrainis and
rebuilt and used by Omanis.* (Dept. Tourism & Antiquities).

Babylon. A report of their visit to Bahrain was written by Alexander's admiral Androsthenes who described his journey in a journal entitled "Voyage along the Indian Coast". He referred to Bahrain as "Tylos" and we are informed that the visit took place in 324 BC. Unfortunately the original report has not survived and our awareness of its contents stem from other Greek sources who depend upon Androsthene's writing for their knowledge of Bahrain. It was used by the Hellenistic geographers Artemidorus and Eratosthenes in their work and botanical information supplied by Androsthenes was drawn on at length by the philosopher Theophrastus. One of the few surviving quotes by Androsthenes concerns his observations on the pearl fishing around Bahrain. He comments that Bahraini pearls were prized throughout the region and observed that the native name for them was "berberi". In a recent paper published in "Bahrain Through The Ages" (1986), G.W. Bowersock points out that this 4th century BC reference to the word "berberi" deserves more attention than it had previously received since at the time of the Roman Empire the Gulf coastal areas (where pearl fishing was a major pursuit) became known as the "Barbary coast".

In the excavation of the ancient cities at Qal'at al Bahrain, evidence has emerged of a Hellenistic period in the last four centuries BC. Pottery from this period was discovered underneath the level of the Islamic fort. It has been suggested that this signifies close links with the Greek empire rather than an occupation by Greeks.

Arad fort. (Dept. Tourism & Antiquities).

The exploration of a supposedly Islamic fort on the shore between the "Portuguese" fortifications and the sea has raised some interesting information concerning Bahrain from the beginning of the Christian era to much more recent times. The fort was apparently built in the latter years of BC or very early AD. We have very little idea of why it was built at this time. There is one reference to a fort existing in Bahrain in the third century AD since it was recorded that King Satirun unsuccessfully defended the fort against the advancing army of the Persian ruler Ardeshire. It s not clear however whether this is the same fort as the one at Qal'at al Bahrain.

Islam was introduced to Bahrain in the 7th century AD at a time when Christianity was already represented on the islands. From 700 AD the islands were ruled, over a period of 350 years, by governors who reported to either Damascus or Baghdad. In 1058 a resident of Bahrain, Abu-l-Bahlul led a rebellion against the Carmarthian rulers, defeating an army sent to crush the revolt. The independence movement was however relatively short lived since Yahya bin Abbas, the Ruler of Qatif, entered the fray and caused Abu-l-Bahlul to flee from the island. This was an extremely turbulent period characterised by recurrent battles and claim of sovereignty by one faction met with counter-claim by another. Eventually, a strong ruler emerged in the form of Abdulla-al-Ayuni who remained in control for many years. The Mosque Suq-Al-Khamis on the Sh.Sulman Highway and the Islamic fort already mentioned survive from this period.

The Portuguese entry into the Indian Ocean following Vasco da Gama's successful rounding of the Cape of Good Hope led to the establishment of military bases at strategic locations throughout the area. Their avowed intention was to control the spice trade routes from India to Europe.

When Portuguese troops captured Hormuz Bahrain became inextricably involved in the conflict since Hormuz demanded homage from Bahrain which, predictably, refused whereupon the island was occupied by Portuguese troops who sailed there from India and from the southern Gulf. The Portuguese fort was built following their occupation of Bahrain in 1521 AD.

In 1529 the Governor of Bahrain decided to follow the example already set by his relative, the Wezir of Hormuz and he too refused to pay taxes. This led to an attack on the island by a small Portuguese fleet which met a series of mishaps, eventually foundering in a storm. In the following years Bahrain formed a buffer zone between the opposing forces of Turkey in the north and Portugal in the south.

The Portuguese were eventually expelled from Bahrain in 1602 as a result of a murderous attack on a Bahrain businessman at the instigation of the Portuguese governor. The victim's relatives wreaked vengeance on the murderer and subsequently a group of local people seized the fort. The insurgents called upon the Persians under Shah Abbas the Great — arch rivals of the Portuguese — for protection whilst successfully staving off a counter-attack on the fort and establishing control of the island. The Persians maintained their authority to a greater or lesser extent until 1718 when they were eventually ousted by Omani forces. Two years later the Persians paid a handsome price to purchase back their control of the island from the Omanis.

In 1783 the islands were captured by the Al Khalifa family. The conquerors laid the foundations of the Al Khalifa dynasty which rules to the present. A brief history of the Al Khalifa family from 1747 to 1986 is given in table II whilst a more recent account of the twentieth century highlights of Bahrain's development can be found in section five.

Above: An Islamic pot, 15th century AD. Left: Islamic pottery; 14th century AD. (Dept. Tourism & Antiquities).

Below: Suq Al-Khamis Mosque is the oldest extant mosque in Bahrain. Opinions concerning it's date of construction vary from those who hold that it was built by the Umayyad Caliph Umar bin Abdul Aziz in 692 AD and those who contend that it is of more recent origins, probably dating to the 11th century. Whichever is correct it is certain that the two minarets are 15th century additions to the original construction. (Dept. Tourism & Antiquities).

	Table I: Historical Summary.

B.P.

8,000	Bahrain's connection with mainland broken. Climate more humid. Man lived around coastline of Gulf and its islands. Depended on sea for food. Ate fish and molluscs which were cooked on open fires. Flint arrow heads. Some dwellings from sandstone slabs.
7,000	Although most settlements were along north coast of Bahrain an attempt made to settle in south-west. This is evidenced by discovery of flint sites 30kms from north coast.
6,000	Some trading established between Mesopotamian cities and settlements of eastern coast of Arabia (i.e. early Dilmun). A temporary settlement at Al Markh off the west coast of Bahrain's main island — used seasonally by fishermen for curing fish. Links with Ubaid based on pottery finds. Early settlers exploited inshore marine resources such as small fish and pearl oysters. Later development of palm boat allowed offshore fishing, including larger fish and even Dugong.
5,000	Man hunted gazelle. 4,800 BP = start of early Bronze Age. Dilmun centred on mainland Arabia. Date of Epic of Gilgamesh put at 2,600 BC. Pearls fished. Burial mounds built on Bahrain. Text dated 2,300 BC: "made the Meluhha ships, the Makkan ships, the Dilmun ships tie up alongside the quayside of Agade." The Trading and ritual centre of Dilmun shifted to Bahrain around 4,250 BP. It entered a vibrant phase of cultural upsurge.
4,000	Cities were built, e.g. Qal'at al Bahrain had approx. 7,000 people. Height of Dilmun civilisation. 150,000 burial mounds over c.500 years. Strong links between Bahrain, Qatif, Dharan and Failaka. Copper trade flourished. By around 3,800 BP Dilmun's importance had waned. There followed a Kassite period when Kilmun known mainly as an exporter of dates. Settlements contracted to the artesian core on north coast.
3,000	Period of increased precipitation and settlements once more spread to south, Dilmun under Babylonian influence. 540 BC Persians conquered islands. 324 BC Alexander the Great's vessels visited Bahrain (Tylos).
2,700	Seleucid period 300 BC to 0.
2,000	Islands of Bahrain peaceful and prosperous. 100 AD Pliny describes Bahrain (Tylos) as being famous for pearls. 200 AD Ptolemy map shows Tylos. Islam introduced to Bahrain. Bahrain ruled by governors on behalf of Caliphs of Damascus and Baghdad.
1,000	1058 AD Abu-l-Bahlul revolted against Carmarthians and declared prince. Wars followed. Bahrain linked with growing maritime trade network. Spice trade. Kingdom of Hormuz at centre of Gulf trade. 1510 Albuquerque: "Bahrain is noted for its large breeding horses; its barley crops; and the variety of its fruits; and all around it are the fishing grounds of seed pearls; and of pearls which are sent to these realms of Portugal, for they are better and more lasting than any that are found in any of these parts". 1507 - 1622 Portuguese control of Hormuz. 1521 - 1602 Portuguese control Bahrain; followed by Persian influence. 1783 Al Khalifa dynasty established (see table II). Early 1900's pearl industry had short revival then declined. Followed by oil and gas discoveries and rapid infrastructural and commercial development. 1986 Saudi Arabia-Bahrain
PRESENT	Causeway officially opened.

	Table II: The Al-Khalifa Dynasty.
1747	Khalifa died and his son Muhammed bin Khalifa migrated to Zubara on west coast of Qatar so that he would be closer to Bahrain pearling industry. He was soon joined by the rest of his family and became well established at Zubara. He used to visit Bahrain on pearl purchasing trips.
1776	Muhammed died and his son Khalifa succeeded him.
1782	Khalifa died while on pilgrimage to Mecca. Ahmed Khalifa who later became known as Ahmed Al Fatih (The Conqueror), took over.
1783	The Persians attacked Zubara and fought against the Al Khalifa, laying seige to the port. Help arrived for Ahmed's cousin the Sabah of Kuwait and Persians were defeated Following this success Ahmed took his following to Bahrain and also defeated the Persians there. Built a strong defensive fleet.
1796	Ahmed al Fatih died, succeeded by two sons; Abdullah and Sulman. Sulman took main interest in Bahrain while Abdullah moved to Saudi Arabia.
1799	Oman again tried to take control of Bahrain. Established a foothold on Muharraq and built Arad fort on south shore. For a while Wahabis occupied Bahrain and Shaikh Sulman bin Ahmed Al-Khalifa retired to the family's old base at Zubara. He eventually returned, following height of pirate period.
1820	Shaikh Sulman returned to Bahrain and he and Abdullah signed "General Treaty" between East India Company and Bahrain.
1825	Shaikh Sulman died — succeeded by his son Khalifa bin Sulman who shared power with his uncle Sheikh Abdullah.
1834	The young nephew Khalifa bin Sulman died — leaving aged Abdullah as sole ruler. Younger family members impatient for progress challenged Abdulla's authority. Great nephew, Muhammed bin Khalifa bin Sulman Al-Khalifa initially controlled Muharraq and then took refuge on Arabian mainland; then to Qatar where he captured fort at Zubara, and finally back to Bahrain in early 1843.
1843	Muhammed gained control of Manama and seiged Abdullah at Abu Mahur fort. Eventually Shaikh Abdullah bin Khalifa surrendered and was exiled.
1848	Abdulla bin Khalifa died in exile in Saudi Arabia.
1861	Treaty of Perpetual Peace and Friendship with British re slavery, maritime aggression and trade.
1864	Son of Shaikh Abdullah, Muhammed bin Abdullah, made several attempts to regain control but was expelled from Damman by British. He remained in region however.
1867	War between Qatari's and Al Khalifa family. Muhammed bin Khalifa fled to Qatar in 1868. Fort at Abu Mahur (Muharraq) destroyed and Bahrain fleet scuttled.
1869	Shaikh Ali Bin Khalifa succeeded as ruler. He was forced to pay 100,000 Maria Theresa dollars for breach of treaty with British. Then Muhammed bin Khalifa invaded Bahrain, killed his brother Ali and became ruller; but was soon deposed by his cousin Muhammed bin Abdullah. The British then returned and deported both of them, finally instating Shaikh Isa (grandson of Khalifa bin Sulman) as ruler of Bahrain. His rule lasted 54 years.
1898	Shaikh Isa appointed his eldest son Shaikh Hamed as Heir apparent.
1902	British Political Agent appointed to Bahrain.
1923	Shaikh Isa abdicated in favour of his son; Shaikh Hamed bin Isa Al Khalifa.
1932	Shaikh Isa died.
1942	Shaikh Hamed died and was succeeded by Shaikh Sulman.
1961	H.H. Shaikh Sulman bin Hamed Al Khalifa died and was succeeded by H.H. Shaikh Isa bin Salman Al Khalifa, the current Amir.

Right: Sailfin Molly: This freshwater fish is common in drainage ditches. (Hill).

Below: Spiny Tailed Lizard (Uromastyx microlepis): *Arabic name 'Dhub': This prehistoric looking lizard is quite common in desert and semi-desert areas. It lives in burrows in the ground or sometimes in crevices under stones and hibernates in winter. As the temperature increases its colour changes from black to yellow. When cornered and alarmed it puffs itself up and hisses aggressively. It is a vegetarian.* (Hill).

Opposite, top: View of the Central Depression and surrounding ridge from the Tree of Life. (Vine).

Opposite, bottom: Blue Pansy (Precis orythia). *This is a fairly common butterfly which occurs in cultivated areas throughout the year.* (Hill).

NATURAL HISTORY

The State of Bahrain consists of thirteen islands and approximately twenty small islets, all of which are situated in a shallow branch of the Arabian Gulf known as the Gulf of Salwa. There are two main groups of islands; i.e. the Bahrain Island-Muharraq-Sitra-Jiddah-Umm Nasan complex which are, with the exception of Jiddah, connected by causeways; and secondly a southern group including Hawar, Sawad and several small islets. A combination of sea-level changes and erosional climatic conditions have wrought their influence upon the landscape. Nowhere is this more apparent than on the main island of Bahrain. The terrain today consists of coastal low-lands, followed by gently inclined slopes terminating in the rim of a crater-like basin known as the Central Depression. This latter feature contains a number of small rocky outcrops or jebels among which is the highest point on the island: Jebel ad-Dukhan. It was not always so.

Geologists refer to the structure of Bahrain as that of an eroded dome, a term best understood by studying the geological cross-section in fig. 3. If one doubts that the entire islands of Bahrain were once covered by sea-water one has only to climb to the top of the highest jebel and to take a look at the rock capping its summit. This rock is composed of a basal conglomerate and fossil corals indicating it was once laid down in shallow water. Indeed, the capping is all that remains of a rock layer which once covered the entire region but has been completely eroded elsewhere.

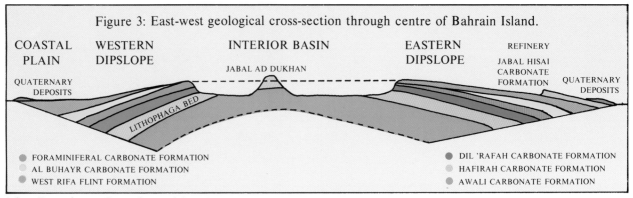

Figure 3: East-west geological cross-section through centre of Bahrain Island.

COASTAL PLAIN   WESTERN DIPSLOPE   INTERIOR BASIN   EASTERN DIPSLOPE   REFINERY

JABAL AD DUKHAN

QUATERNARY DEPOSITS

JABAL HISAI CARBONATE FORMATION   QUATERNARY DEPOSITS

LITHOPHAGA BED

● FORAMINIFERAL CARBONATE FORMATION
○ AL BUHAYR CARBONATE FORMATION
○ WEST RIFA FLINT FORMATION

● DIL 'RAFAH CARBONATE FORMATION
○ HAFIRAH CARBONATE FORMATION
○ AWALI CARBONATE FORMATION

(after Doornkamp, Brunsden and Jones).

A recent study of geomorphic evidence for sea-level changes has provided a more comprehensive picture. At the time of the last interglacial period (i.e. 125,000 to 80,000 years ago) sea-level was four to five metres higher than at present. During this period most of Bahrain's main island was underwater. The few outcrops of land which did form islands were uninhabited, barren and rugged with no supplies of fresh-water since the areas of springs along today's north coast of Bahrain were several metres below sea-level. Following this interglacial era a glacial period ensued during which the sea-level fell dramatically so that most of the previous sea-bed of the Arabian Gulf became dry-land. Erstwhile islands of the Bahrain group were thus connected to the Arabian subcontinent and the fresh-water springs disgorged over land instead of under-water. The coastline of the Gulf region lay to the south, along the perimeter of present day Gulf of Oman. During this long period the climate was much cooler and one may assume that the low lands of the Gulf were relatively verdant. At the end of the glacial period sea-level rose once more and surpassed its present level, but this time by not so much as during the previous interglacial period. For around two thousand years, from 7,000 BP to 5,000 BP the sea around Bahrain was about two metres above today's level. Since that time there have been further sea level changes which, although over an amplitude of as little as two metres, have exerted important influences upon the natural history of the island and consequently upon Man. Apart from the obvious effects which a shift in sea-level has upon the location of coastal settlements, harbours and jetties, the rise and fall of water also affected the availability of ground water suitable for irrigation or drinking since saline penetration of shallow levels was significantly increased by a sea level rise of one metre.

An investigation of archaeological remains on Bahrain, dating back to around four thousand years ago, has provided evidence of more recent fluctuations in sea-level, summarised in fig. 4.

The fortuitous presence of fresh-water sources of Bahrain's main island must be the single most important influence on both Man's presence over the millenia and on the island's natural history. Some of these life-giving springs disgorge onto land while others are now sited below sea-level and thus empty their valuable fresh-water into the sea. For thousands of years Man and nature have harmoniously co-existed in this unique environment. Although modern development of a country such as Bahrain inevitably

causes a great strain on the preservation of natural habitats it will interest the reader to learn how wildlife has been preserved and what measures the Government has taken to ensure the protection of its most important heritage — the natural and renewable resources of the Bahrain islands.

It is true that the initial impression of the Bahrain countryside may be one of an arid desert apparently devoid of life. To many transient visitors this observation is hard to dispel whereas in fact Bahrain is a naturalist's paradise composed of rare and fascinating plants and animals together with unique seasonal migrations of breeding populations of birds.

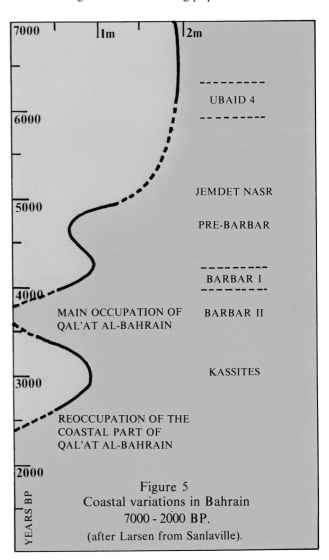

7000   1m   2m

UBAID 4

6000

JEMDET NASR

5000

PRE-BARBAR

BARBAR I

4000

MAIN OCCUPATION OF QAL'AT AL-BAHRAIN   BARBAR II

KASSITES

3000

REOCCUPATION OF THE COASTAL PART OF QAL'AT AL-BAHRAIN

2000

YEARS BP

Figure 5
Coastal variations in Bahrain
7000 - 2000 BP.

(after Larsen from Sanlaville).

Bahrain's famous "Tree of Life". (Vine).

My own conversion to that inner circle of nature lovers initiated in the delights of Bahrain and its rewarding natural environment occurred one March afternoon when my guide, Elsa Cook, had taken me to see the famous "Tree of Life". We had driven past Awali and zig-zagged our way across the oil-fields; down into the Central Depression. Fascinated to learn why a tree had been accredited with such nobility, I scrutinised the terrain as we headed towards what, at first sight, seemed to be barren desert. Not alone were there no trees to be seen, but there was little sign of scrub bushes or other vegetation. "Ah! There it is", Elsa assured me and I searched the landscape in the direction she was indicating. Sure enough, about a mile away, a lone tree was silhouetted against the skyline. Since it was the only one in sight I had no difficulty in believing Elsa's identification of it as "The Tree of Life". We took the rough track leading in that general direction and parked about a hundred metres away so that I could walk the last stretch up a sandy hillock to admire the huge Acacia which had inexplicably succeeded in flourishing in this incredibly harsh environment. Out there, in the midst of expansive desert, one's senses became finely attuned to the raw beauty of nature. Standing beneath the spreading, swaying branches I listened to the tree's heartbeat of rustling leaves and the creaks of old age. Towards its base, a number of roots splayed out from the gnarled trunk before delving underground. Among the branches, small birds rested and a quick search revealed a solitary nest.

Magnificent though it is (and well worth visiting), the "Tree of Life" was not the only thing which impressed me as I lingered beneath its canopy. Located towards the middle of Bahrain's Central Depression, and situated on a slight rise, it gives one a perfect view of the surrounding desert with, in the distance, the jagged rim of the crater clearly visible. By the time I was ready to leave, the sun was already setting and I realised that the hour or so spent on that isolated mound had crystallised my entire feelings about Bahrain — what had begun as mild interest and a vague sensation of "belonging" — had evolved into a much deeper love for its unique range of characteristics and a determination to become more closely acquainted with its natural history.

Bahrain's climate has, of course, played a major role in the shaping of its wildlife profile. December to March, the winter months, temperatures are coolest and winds blow from the north and north-west. The annual average rainfall is approximately 77 millimetres and March is the wettest month. Both monthly and annual figures for rainfall show wide variation and about the only consistent feature is that April to October are extremely dry months when little or no rain is ever recorded. The pattern of temperatures (table III) shows less variation from year to year. Average daily temperatures in

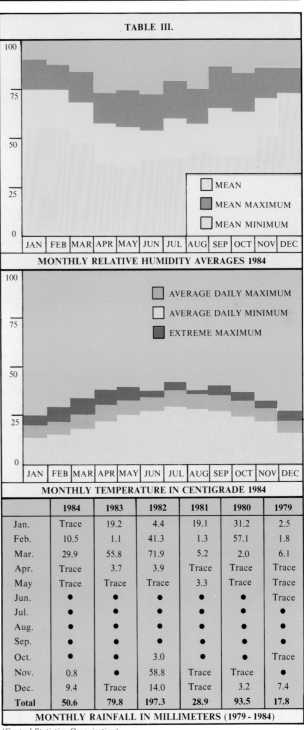

TABLE III.

MONTHLY RELATIVE HUMIDITY AVERAGES 1984

- ☐ MEAN
- ☐ MEAN MAXIMUM
- ☐ MEAN MINIMUM

MONTHLY TEMPERATURE IN CENTIGRADE 1984

- ☐ AVERAGE DAILY MAXIMUM
- ☐ AVERAGE DAILY MINIMUM
- ☐ EXTREME MAXIMUM

	1984	1983	1982	1981	1980	1979
Jan.	Trace	19.2	4.4	19.1	31.2	2.5
Feb.	10.5	1.1	41.3	1.3	57.1	1.8
Mar.	29.9	55.8	71.9	5.2	2.0	6.1
Apr.	Trace	3.7	3.9	Trace	Trace	Trace
May	Trace	Trace	Trace	3.3	Trace	Trace
Jun.	•	•	•	•	•	Trace
Jul.	•	•	•	•	•	•
Aug.	•	•	•	•	•	•
Sep.	•	•	•	•	•	•
Oct.	•	•	3.0	•	•	Trace
Nov.	0.8	•	58.8	Trace	Trace	•
Dec.	9.4	Trace	14.0	Trace	3.2	7.4
Total	50.6	79.8	197.3	28.9	93.5	17.8

MONTHLY RAINFALL IN MILLIMETERS (1979 - 1984)

(Central Statistics Organisation).

Below, left: A surviving copse of the mangrove Avicennia
marina. *(Vreeland).*

*Below, right: The land of Bahrain was once covered by sea.
Today the floor of the Central Depression bears open testament
to its geological past. (Vine).*

winter are around 12 - 15 degrees centigrade while
this rises to approximately 25 in July and August
(mean daily minimum: January = 15; mean daily
maximum: August = 38). Daily temperatures in
summer are influenced by wind direction with the
cool north "Barih" bringing some welcome but
generally short-lived relief during June and the less
welcome "Qaws" which blows from the south being
interspersed with a moist north-westerly "shamal".

In order to discuss the distribution of wildlife on the
main island of Bahrain it is first necessary to
acknowledge its demarcation into four major regions
briefly described below.

THE ENVIRONMENT OF THE MAIN ISLAND
1. The Northern Plain.

The northern region of Bahrain and the linked
islands of Al Muharraq and Sitra form a low plateau,
seldom more than three metres above sea level. The
low coastal tract supports a thin covering of sand and
marine debris overlying old beachrock or limestone.
About 50m inshore thicker sand deposits mark a
previous coastline and shifting sand forms a dune
ridge which reaches 15m above sea-level. Towards the
south, the ground slopes gradually away from the
ridge into an area drained by tributaries of the stream
fed by Khadra pool and which enters the sea via the
Khawr Tubli estuary.

Sediment has accumulated on this northern plain as
a result of previous mangrove swamps — important
contributors to coastline consolidation. The clay-
loam soil thus created overlies sand. The main dunes
have accumulated on the north-west coastline.
Geological studies have indicated that the sand from
which the dunes are comprised originated on the
Arabian mainland from whence it blew across to
Bahrain during the Pleistocene period when sea-level
was much lower than it is today. East of Sar, in an area
of low-lying ground, gypsum and sand-dunes occur
and, as a result of the presence of ground water only
60 - 70 cms beneath the surface, these are
consolidated by vegetation.

2. Escarpments and Back-slopes.

A rim, rising to around 50m above sea-level
surrounds the Central Depression of Bahrain. From
outside of the depression this rim is almost
indiscernible since the land rises gradually from the
coast to reach the rim-crest. At that point however, it
suddenly dips down to the floor of the concavity and
viewed from the inside the rim is a most distinctive
feature of the landscape. The back-slopes which
stretch from the rim to the coastal plain vary in width
fom two to three kilometers wide and they are
covered with loose stones, scoured here and there by
flood drainage channels.

3. The Central Depression.

The interior basin of Bahrain is not all low ground.
In fact the highest point of the island: Jebel ad-
Dukhan (122m above sea level) arises from the floor
of the depression and resembles, as a result of its
eroded horizontal rocky strata, a worn down table
mountain. During periods of rainfall, rivulets drain off
the Jebel and flow towards the low ground, close to
the crater rim before disappearing underground.

4. The Sabkhas — Salt-Mud flats

The southern coast of Bahrain is formed by a low
sandy plain which supports little vegetation since
ground-water is highly saline. Beach ridges are
formed from sand, marine debris and large quantities
of empty gastropod *(Cerithium)* shells.

A recent study of soil types occuring on the island
has identified four main groups; i.e. Solonchaks;
Regosols; Vermosols and Fluvisols. Without entering
into a detailed discussion regarding the soil-types of
Bahrain it is worth noting that the country has a
remarkable variety of forms of gypsum accumulation
despite the fact that there is very little gypsum in the
underlying strata. The accumulations can be
explained by the continuous upwellings of sulphate
rich ground water since the last pluvial period.

Bahrain's dates are still regarded as among the most delicious to be found anywhere. The method of harvesting has changed little over the centuries. (Falcon).

VEGETATION — PLANT-LIFE

Despite the high gypsum content of its soil, Bahrain has succeeded in a number of agricultural ventures where suitable irrigation water is available. One example is that of the date-palm *(Phoenix dactylifera),* locally known as "Nakhale". It has been successfully cultivated on the island since its presumed introduction from neighbouring countries several thousand years ago. A study of the date-palm in Bahrain has reported that over 400,000 trees were being actively grown on the island in recent years but that numbers are in decline. The main problem has been an increase in salinity of ground-water and shortages of good quality water for irrigation purposes. Nevertheless, the general climatic conditions on Bahrain seem to suit the date palm which requires hot and dry weather for crop ripening with low rainfall during the flowering period. Extra high humidity may result in dates wilting and falling off the trees while consistent hot and dry winds during the ripening period cause very hard dates. Prolonged frost can also kill the trees.

As a source of food, dates have played an important role in the lives of Bahrainis since earliest recorded civilisation. Dates were one of the principle recorded products of Dilmun and were renowned, even then, for their sweetness. They were regarded as a

particularly suitable offering to the gods. Writing in their report to the Royal Geographic Society of a visit to Bahrain towards the end of the last century, Theodore Bent commented as follows:

> "Green dates (salang) are given to the donkeys for fodder, and to this the Bahraini attribute their exceptionally good breed. They make "sheerah" for their own consumption out of dates dried for three days; then date-juice is poured over them and sesame seeds, walnuts, or ginger powder mixed with them. For exportation the dates are dried and the date juice allowed to run-off in the "madabash", and then they are packed in date-leaf baskets. To manure their date-groves they use the fins of a species of ray-fish called "awal", which, by the way, was an ancient name of the island of Bahrain".

The date palm itself is one of the best utilised of cultivated plants. Apart from the dates which are consumed, other parts of the plant are well used. The trunk is employed in building temporary structures and barasti buildings, while the leaflets provide the raw material for weaving a variety of products including fans, mats and baskets. The central axis of the fronds is used for construction of poultry baskets, cages and for fencing. Rope is made from the fibres drawn from the base of the trunk while other parts may be used as fuel for cooking or heating.

In addition to the date palm cultivation along the north and north-west of Bahrain a number of other crops are farmed there including alfalfa, tomatoes, cabbages, cauliflowers, lettuce, carrots, onions, egg-plants, beetroot, turnips, potatoes, snake-cucumbers, water-melons, cantaloups, okra, marrow and pumpkin. In 1984 5,556 donums were under vegetable crop production and they yielded 7,437 tons of vegetables. Data on agricultural activities taking place, mainly in the north of the islands, is given in table III.

TABLE IV.

ESTIMATED PRODUCTION OF DIFFERENT VEGETABLE CROPS BY WEIGHT AND VALUE (1982/83 — 1983/84).

CROPS	Value in Thousand BD.		Production in Tons		Area in Dounum	
	1983/84	1982/83	1983/84	1982/83	1983/84	1982/83
Tomatoes	973	1,078	3,537	3,089	1,901.68	1,919.88
Cabbage	149	87	484	402	236.88	196.36
Cauliflower	53	38	213	149	200.13	127.99
Lettuce	120	118	504	524	252.09	262.20
Carrots	110	78	299	291	200.85	195.53
Onions (Green)	42	86	392	552	130.61	183.92
Eggplants	49	58	172	167	106.99	103.53
Beetroot	2	4	13	22	35.90	16.53
Turnips	8	16	49	79	55.19	46.76
Potatoes	8	5	45	26	27.22	16.05
Snake Cucumber	152	255	332	484	342.69	498.89
Watermelons	—	—	—	—	51.28	76.56
Cantaloups	9	5	34	26	516.64	409.85
Okra	23	32	45	49	239.26	263.77
Marrow	138	175	657	527	382.15	272.33
Pumpkin	27	12	132	46	68.72	23.92
Other Vegetables	97	62	529	480	808.34	613.72
Total	**1,960**	**2,109**	**7,437**	**6,913**	**5,556.62**	**5,227.79**

(Central Statistics Organisation).

Zygophyllum qaterense: *A perennial plant with fleshy stems and leaves forming compact low and rounded bushes. The flowers are pale yellow and are formed in February - April. The plants are grazed by camels. Probably the commonest and most widespread plant on the island.* (Hill).

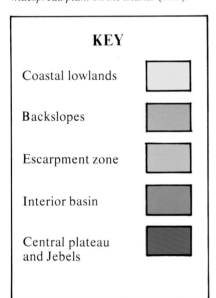

KEY

Coastal lowlands

Backslopes

Escarpment zone

Interior basin

Central plateau and Jebels

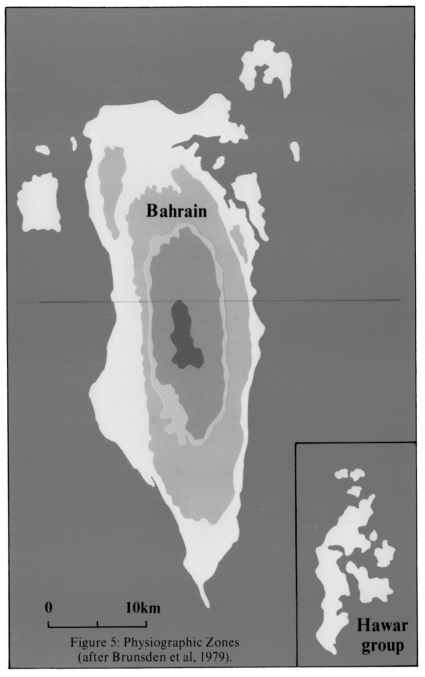

Figure 5: Physiographic Zones
(after Brunsden et al, 1979).

Despite this intensive cultivation, Bahrain has retained an interesting assemblage of wild plants and the island provides an opportunity to study species inhabiting a wide variety of habitats. The floral affinites are with plants from North Africa and India and no endemic species have so far been recorded. Conditions for plant growth are, as I have already intimated, quite harsh since they must withstand the extreme heat and dryness of summer months while maintaining their hold in saline soils with their extra high gypsum content.

The naturally occuring wild plants are therefore for the most part halophytes (salt-loving) or xerophytes (drought resistant) while some are able to derive all their moisture from the underlying water table (phreatophytes). Each type of habitat on the islands have their own characteristic group of plants referred to by botanists as the phytal association.

The Northern Plain, as we have seen, has highly saline soils with a particularly high gypsum content. Not surprisingly, halophytic plants are the main kind colonising the area but there are several phytal associations which occur in the various habitats. These are summarised below.

PLANT ASSOCIATIONS
Loam Plains: *Suaeda vermiculata — Cressa cretica* Association.

Intricately branched bushes of the perennial shrub: *Suaeda vermiculata* ("Gadgad") are a frequent sight along the northerly coastal plain of Bahrain, especially among abandoned date palm groves where it may form an undergrowth of tangled thickets. Its petioled, fleshy leaves are browsed by camels. Found in the same area, often growing between bushes of "gadgad" are small upright stems of the perennial

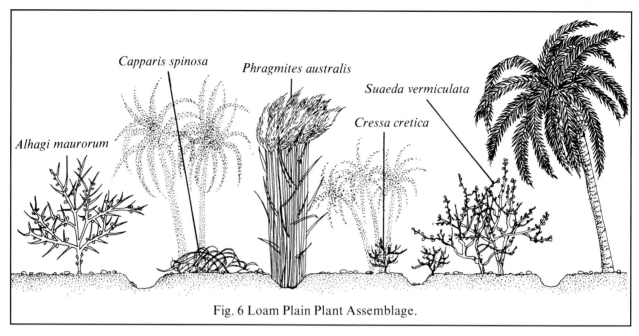

Fig. 6 Loam Plain Plant Assemblage.

herb: *Cressa cretica,* known locally as "Shuwal". Fine hairs cover the stem and closely packed leaves.

Both species predominate on silty and loamy soils where the water table is high. Other species occuring in this association include *Capparis spinosa,* the "Caper" (locally known as "Dabayyi") is a perennial, forming thickets of sprawling branches with edible flower buds known as "capers". One may also find in these loamy soils of the northern plain the green thorny bush *Alhagi maurorum* or Heidji; and reed grass, *Phragmites australis,* also called "Gaspa" which is common in water-logged soil and superficially resembles Garden Pampas grass.

Khadara Depression: *Halocnemum strobilaceum — — Suaeda vermiculata* Association.

Depressions in the region around Aali village; Ain al Khadara and Salmabad consist of saline, gypsic soils sparsely colonised by stunted bushes of *Suaeda vermiculata* and scattered clumps of the fleshy stemmed perennial *Halocnemum stobilaceum* ("Toof"). Other plants occurring in the association include *Salsola baryosma* ("Ramram"); the perennial grass *Aeluropus littoralis;* the tall rush *Juncus acutus* ("Asal") and the succulent shrublet *Halopeplis perfoliata.*

Tidal swamps: *Arthrocnemum glaucum — Avicennia marina* Association.

The dwarf mangrove, *Avicennia marina,* living here at the northern extremity of its range, has played a major part in consolidation of coastal terrain and in creating important shallow-water or inter-tidal habitats. Unfortunately it has suffered greatly due to land reclamation and coastal pollution. Nevertheless, it does survive along the banks of some drainage channels and sheltered lagoons. It is this habitat, perhaps more than any other, which is seriously threatened by development projects and there is a case to be made for protection of the remaining tidal swamps and their wild-life.

The water-logged, highly saline mud in which the mangroves are anchored supports relatively few other plants but several do occur in this harsh environment. They embrace the succulent, low sprawling bushes of *Arthrocnemum glaucum;* the erect succulent *Salicornia herbacea; Halocnemum strobilaceum;* reed-grass; *Phragmites australis;* "Rijla"; *Suaeda maritima* and a species of rush: *Juncus* sp.

Nebkha Plain Plant assemblage: *Zygophyllum qatarense — Anabasis articulata* Association.

The Nebka plain is covered by soils of relatively low

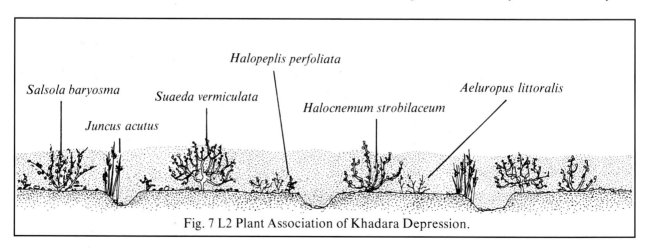

Fig. 7 L2 Plant Association of Khadara Depression.

Halopeplis perfoliata: *This odd looking plant is common in areas of high salinity, particularly along the shoreline. The leaf rudiments are almost spherical and minute yellow flowers protrude from the joints. It flowers April to May.* (Hill).

salinity but with a high gypsum content. It is a generally well drained area in which the water-table lies about two metres beneath the surface. Most plants occuring there depend on this for their moisture control (i.e. phreatophytes) and species include: compact shrubs of the succulents *Zygophyllum qatarense* and *Anabasis articulata* which are grazed by camels. Other species comprise the straggly ground shrub *Atriplex leucoclada* and densely branched bushes of *Suaeda vermiculata* together with the grasses *Aeluropus lagopoides; Sporobulus arabicus* and the conspicuous rush *Juncus acutus.*

Northern Sand Sheets: *Helioptropium crispum —
Salsola baryosma* Association.

The aeolian sand sheet extending west of Maqabah and south, past Sar and towards Buddayya consists of dry, low salinity sandy soil in which typically xerophytic plant species occur. Characteristic species include the greyish, hairy leafed ground shrub "Fohah" *(Heliotropium crispum)* and tangled clumps of the fleshy leafed ground shrub: "Ramram" *(Salsola baryosma)*. Other members of the association include the dwarf perennial sedge *Cyperus arenarius;* the thorny shrub "Jambut" *(Prosopis farcata)* which is especially common in abandoned irrigation areas; and the resilient perennial grass "Nedjma" *(Sporobulus arabicus)*. The thorny tree known locally as "Shahass" or "Mesquite" *(Prosopis juliflora)* — a South American introduction to Bahrain — occurs sporadically within this association, forming small thickets or as isolated trees. Low, bushy clumps of *Phoenix dactylifera* also occur here as does the tussock grass *Pennisetum divisum.*

Al Areen Sand Sheets: *Sporobolus arabicus —
Helianthemum lippii* Association.

The Al Areen Wildlife Sanctuary occurs within this area which extends along the west coast of Bahrain from Zallaq to Al Areen. The water table is somewhat higher than occurs under the northern sand sheets described above but gypsum content of the soil is also higher. There is approximately twenty percent ground cover created by dwarf perennial xerophytes and

phreatophytes. A conspicuous species within the sanctuary is the broom bush: *Leptadenia pyrotechnica* which reaches a height of 2m. A list of plants recorded from the sanctuary is given in table V.

Table V. LIST OF PLANTS IN AL AREEN WILDLIFE SANCTUARY.	
Asclepiadaceae	*Leptadenia pyrotechnica*
Boraginaceae	*Arnebia decumbens*
	Heliotropium crispum
Caryophyllaceae	*Polycarpea repens*
Cistaceae	*Helianthemum lippii*
Compositae	*Launea mucronata*
	Atractylis flava
Cyperaceae	*Cyperus arenarius*
	Cyperus conglomeratus
Geraniaceae	*Monsonia nivea*
Gramineae	*Panicum turgidum*
	Pennisetum divisum
	Erempogon foveolatus
	Stipagrostis ciliata
	Schismus barbatus
	Aeluropus lagopoides
	Sporobolus arabicus
Juncaceae	*Juncus acutus*
Polygonaceae	*Calligonum polygonoides*
Solanaceae	*Lycium shawii*
Zygophyllaceae	*Fagonia indica*
	Zygophyllum qatarense
	Zygophyllum simplex

(The above list is reproduced from : K.J. Virgo, B.N.H.S. Ann. Rep. 1978 - 79).

Left: Limmonium axillare: *Arabic name 'Wagal': A colourful perennial herb which flowers from December to April and grows on a wide range of soils from wet saline to dry rocky hillsides.* (Hill).

Below: Fagonia indica: *Arabic name 'Agoul': A perennial thorny plant which forms straggly clumps. Pale mauve flowers from March to June. Common in dry sandy areas.* (Hill).

Western Coastal Sabkhas: *Zygophyllum qatarense — Halopeplis perfoliata* Association.

The south and south-west coast of Bahrain consists of low sandy areas in which beach ridges and shell banks occur. The soil is extremely saline and gypsic and not surprisingly, there are few plants which have successfully colonised the region. A notable exception is the widespread low, bushy perennial with its purple shiny stems and dark green spherical succulent leaves: *Zygophyllum qatarense.* The shore-line ridge, a short distance above high tide mark, has a dense cover of the succulent chenopod *Halopeplis perfoliata* and the bushy shrub *Seidlitzia rosmarinus* whose pale green succulent leaves are grazed by camels.

Eastern Coastal Sabkhas — *Halopeplis amplexicaulis — Halocnemum strobilaceum* Association.

Coastal sand-flats along the east coast have fine grained sandy-soil and generally a higher salinity than those along the west coast. Dominant plants are the halophytic species: *Halopeplis amplexicaulis Halocnemum strobilaceum* and *Suaeda vermicuata.*

Irrigated areas — Weeds.

Agricultural development has resulted in the introduction of a number of weeds which originate from the cooler regimes. Once irrigation ceases these are soon replaced by indigenous salt tolerant species.

Table V provides a list of common weeds occuring in gardens and among irrigated fields in Bahrain.

Backslopes — *Salsola vermiculata — Erempogon foveolatus.*

These have been briefly described on page 38. The ground is covered by stone pavements or very shallow stony soils. The water table is too far below the surface for it to provide moisture requirements and most plants are therefore xerophytes.

Salsola vermiculata is a straggly woody xerophytic perennial shrub which is seldom more than 50cms in height. It usually appears to be dead or dying since its leaves are tiny and are distributed in widely spaced clusters along the stem. *Erempogon foveolatus* is a perennial grass growing in tufts in dry, sandy areas.

Other species within the association include low bushy growths of *Hammada elegans;* the succulent ground shrub *Anabasis articulata;* the sea lavender *Limonium axillare;* the bushy perennial *Zygophyllum qaterense* and the Euphorbid shrublet *Andrachne telephoides.* Flash-flood stream beds have the dwarf shrub *Cassia italica* and trees of *Acacia tortilis* also occur, particularly along the south-western base of the backslopes.

Central Depression.

The central basin embodies a variety of substrata and soil types including drainage channels, alluvial fans, sand sheets, sabkhas and rock platforms. For the most part, plant-life is relatively sparse and comprises xerophytes such as *Zygophyllum qatarense; Z. simplex; Heliotropium crispum; Fagonia indica; Helianthemum lippii* and *Calligonum polygonoides.* The flora of sand sheets is similar to that occuring in the Al Areen sanctuary while the alluvial fans are endowed with the plants *Herniaria hemistemon, Euphorbia densa* and *Asphodelus tenuifolius.*

Central Plateau — Jebels — Escarpment

High ground on Bahrain consists of bare rock terrain with isolated pockets of soil. Plant-life is relatively scarce but includes *Ochradenus baccatus; Limonium axillare, Andrachne telephoides; Helianthemum lippi; Tetrapogon villosus; Glossonema edule* and *Calligonum polygonoides.*

Top left: Red Thumb (Cynomorium coccineum): *This fungus-like plant carries many minute crimson flowers clustered around a single stalk. It is found in sandy areas in January and February. In some years it is more in evidence than in others.* (Hill).

Top right: Desert or Arabian Primrose (Arnebia decumbens): *Arabic name 'Kheel': This plant belongs to the Forget-me-not family. The red root is used by Bedouin women as rouge. It flowers in Spring.* (Hill).

Left: Lycium shawi; *the Desert Thorn is common on Hawar islands where it is distinguished by its red berries.* (Vine).

Below left: Desert Hyacinth: Yellow Broomrape (Cistanche phelipaea): *This plant is parasitic on the goosefoot family. It flowers every January to March.* (Hill).

Below right: Red lantern (Calligonum polygonoides): *Arabic name — 'Abal': A woody shrub which grows upto 1.5m high. The main stem is woody. Flowers which occur during March — April are delicate, pink, and occur in clusters. The fruit is rusty red with hairy edges. Found mainly in stony deserts of the interior of Bahrain. It is sometimes used for firewood.* (Hill).

Dolphins lead the way between coastal reefs off Bahrain's east coast. (Vine).

THE MARINE ENVIRONMENT

Above all else, Bahrain is a group of islands set in a shallow, yet highly productive sea. The marine environment has played a vital role in the development of the island, principally by providing Bahrainis with a natural barrier against invasion; but also by acting as a vital source of food; a treasure chest of pearls generating considerable wealth for the inhabitants and as a channel of communication and trade with distant lands. It is not surprising therefore that Bahrain preserves a strong maritime tradition and is justifiably proud of its coastal waters. In recent years the sea around Bahrain, has been utilised in a number of new ways — embracing the provision of drinking water from desalination plants and of cooling water for industrial plants; the supply of economic fill material for land reclamation and simultaneous deepening of channels or harbours; the location of a land-link between Saudi Arabia and Bahrain and a sporting playground. Bahrain's marine environment has been placed under considerable strain as a result of such rapid developments and increased utilisation but the shallow waters of the Arabian Gulf are still a rich natural resource where a range of marine habitats continue to exist and, in some cases, to flourish.

Bahrain is situated in the Gulf of Salwa, a section of the Arabian Gulf which is itself part of the Arabian Sea and is linked to it via the Strait of Hormuz and the Gulf of Oman. The Arabian Gulf has an average depth of only 35m and most of the Bahrain section is much shallower than this. As a consequence the effects of high evaporation rates, caused by wind and heat, have a considerable influence on both salinity and temperatures of Gulf waters. In shallow areas salt concentration can reach levels as high as 70 ppt (parts per thousand) while the main body of water varies

from 37 ppt to 40 ppt compared with normal oceanic water of 36 ppt. Temperatures also show rapid and marked fluctuations with a seasonal range in shallow areas of around 14 degrees Centigrade in winter rising to 38 in summer. The seasonal temperature range in offshore water is 13 to 31 degrees centigrade.

Tidal currents in the Gulf play an important part in scouring channels and in mixing sea-water. The vertical tidal range of around 80 cms is not all that large but current velocities may exceed 60cms/sec and thus play a significant role in transportation of planktonic organisms and in general water exchange. Recent studies have revealed the pattern of tidal currents occuring around Bahrain. Between low and high tide the current off the east coast flows southwards, with the flow concentrated in the channels on each side of the fasht (see figures 8 and 9). This tidal movement brings less saline water to Ras al Bar and Hawar Islands. Following high tide, as the ebb commences, the flow is reversed and more saline water is carried away from the northern side of Dawhat Salwah. Thus, tidal flows, north and south, off the east coast of Bahrain result in regular sharp changes in salinity at a particular location and resident marine-life must be able to deal with the physical stress involved. Diurnal changes in salinity caused by tidal exchange can be as great as 7 ppt near Ras al Bar while variations of only 1 ppt occur north of the Fasht.

Off the west coast of Bahrain the flooding tide carries less saline water into the Gulf of Bahrain while the ebb tide has the reverse effect, removing higher salinity waer. The salinity fluctuations thus caused are around 4 ppt (in the area between Al Aziziyah and Um Nasan). These effects are summarised in figures 8 and 9.

A recent survey of Bahrain's marine environment has been conducted by the country's Environmental Protection Technical Secretariat (EPTS) using the most modern methods including satellite imagery. I spoke to Walter Vreeland from the EPTS who explained to me what is involved in this project.

"In 1985 we undertook a study of the critical marine habitats within Bahrain's waters. The purpose of this study was to identify, characterize and map the important marine habitats in order to identify areas of importance that could be adversely affected by land reclamation projects and pollution. The study was funded by the Regional Organization for the Protection of the Marine Environment (ROPME) of which Bahrain is a member state.

"ERSAC, in Scotland, under contract to the EPTS, obtained and processed data from the U.S. National Oceanographic and Atmospheric Administration's Landstat V satellite to produce an initial habitat map. Landstat V is in a sun synchronous orbit at a nominal height of 705 k. We used a Thematic Mapper (TM) scanner which has a ground resolution of 30m by 30m (one pixel) and scans 7 different wavelength bands. Bands 1, 2 and 3 were extracted and enhanced to provide information on water depths and marine habitats. After production of the initial habitat map the EPTS surveyed 234 coastal and offshore sites to provide ground-truthing data for verification and final production of the map. Each site was surveyed for depth, bottom type, grain size analysis, organic

content, information on species distribution and water quality. Data from each site were then compared against the data in the 25 map pixels representing that site. The analysis showed a 90% correlation between actual data and satellite data.

"This study has demonstrated that the use of remote sensing for habitat mapping is an extremely useful tool. Data retrieved from future satellite passes can be analyzed to determine seasonal changes in habitats as well as long term changes due to natural or man-made causes."

Having been convinced of the value of this ultra-modern approach to marine biological research I asked Walter Vreeland whether it would be possible to see the resulting satellite imagery of Bahrain's coastal waters. I am indebted to him and to the Environmental Protection Secretariat for permission to reproduce the photograph on page 48.

The shallow marine habitats, or biotopes, of great significance around the Bahrain are as follows:
  (a) Intertidal areas including mud-flats, sand flats and tidal creeks.
  (b) Soft, sub-tidal sea-bed.
  (c) Sea grass beds.
  (d) Coral reefs.
  Coral reefs or offshore banks are known as "Fasht" while the deeper areas are called "Hayr".
  Intertidal areas in those regions where salinity is relatively low have high levels of benthic productivity

Figure 8: Mean salinity levels around Bahrain approaching slack water on a rising tide.

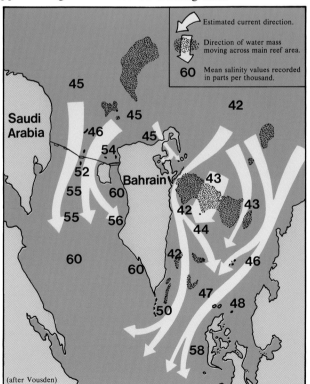

Figure 9: Mean salinity levels around Bahrain approaching slack water on a falling tide.

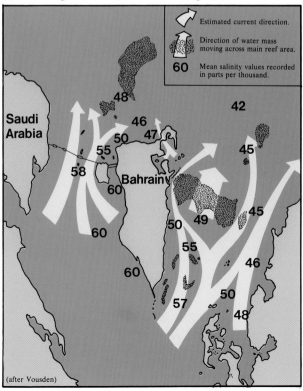

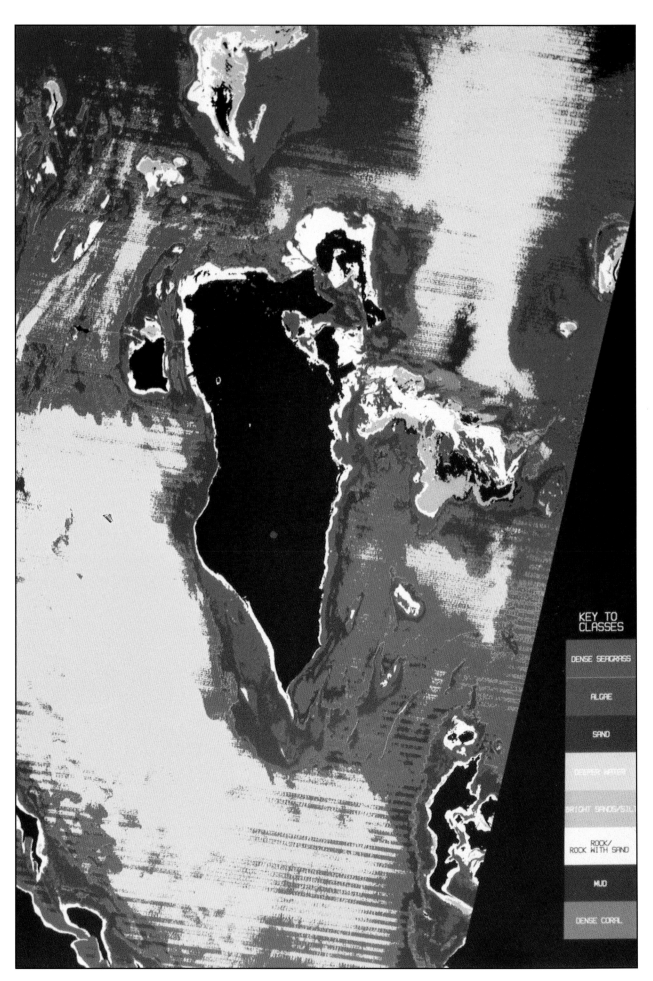

KEY TO
CLASSES

DENSE SEAGRASS

ALGAE

SAND

DEEPER WATER

BRIGHT SANDS/SILT

ROCK/
ROCK WITH SAND

MUD

DENSE CORAL

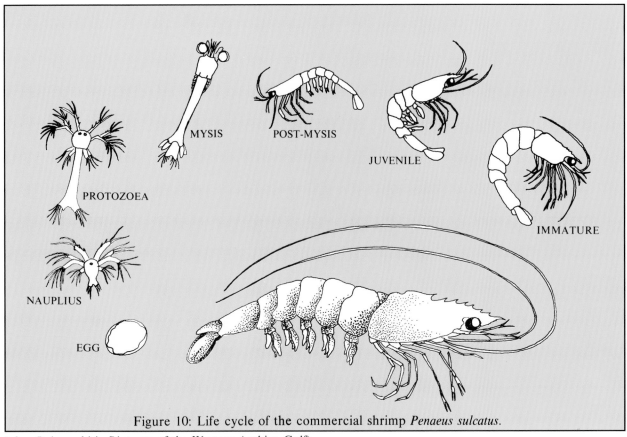

Figure 10: Life cycle of the commercial shrimp *Penaeus sulcatus.*

(after Bobrowski in Biotopes of the Western Arabian Gulf).
and are exploited, during high tide, by many fish and shellfish. Another study carried out by staff of Bahrain's E.P.T.S. illustrates this quite clearly. Marine scientist David Vousden reported that a single haul of a 20m long beach seine across 80m of intertidal mudflat yielded a mixed catch of 1200 juvenile and adult fish and 600 juvenile shrimps.

During 1984 five thousand six hundred tons of sea food, caught in Bahraini waters, were landed on the island. About 18% of this (985 tons) was high value crustaceans (shrimps, crabs and shovel lobsters). In 1985, the catch rose to 7,463 tons. Bahraini shrimps, *Penaeus semisulcatus* are, in the author's view, among the most delicious to be found anywhere in the world. Their populations are sensitive to depletion resulting from over-fishing, pollution, or destruction of their nursery areas. Like many animals, they occupy a range of habitats at various stages of their lives and damage to just one of these can affect the entire life-cycle of the species and bring about a collapse in its population. *Penaeus semisulcatus* breeds in early spring when spawning females discharge thousands of already fertilised eggs into the sea, generally under the protection of darkness. These drift in the plankton for about a day before hatching into pear-shaped nauplii larvae which are active swimmers. They develop via a series of moults into protozoa larvae feeding on phytoplankton. A further series of moults

produces the carnivorous mysis larvae feeding on zooplankton. Three more moults bring the developing shrimp to the post mysis stage which eventually settle to the bottom to become juvenile shrimps. The whole planktonic phase lasts about three weeks.

Commercial fishing carried out in Bahrain waters provides a good indication of the richness of its marine environment. The resource has been well managed by the Bahrain government and shrimp catches have recently recovered as a result of imposing closed fishing seasons during the spring breeding season and through strict control of fishing effort through a system of licensing fishermen. Apart from the shrimps, commented on above, the catch includes a wide range of fish and shellfish species. These are summarised in table VI.

The most significant fish species, in terms of quantities landed are, for the artisinal fisheries, Siganids (Rabbit fish) and for the commercial fisheries, Trevallies. Seafoods are sold to Bahrainis and other residents at Manama's fish market where a vast range of species are on display at numerous stalls. The different kinds of fish are distinguished by their local Arabic names. Thus, the Lethrinid snapper *(Lethrinus lentjan)* is called "Sharee"; "Hamour" is the popular gouper species (questionably identified as *Epinephelus tauvina),* and rabbit-fish are known as "Saffee". A more complete listing is given on page 52.

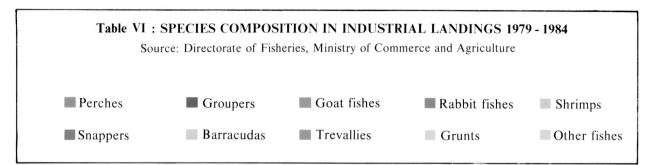

Table VI : SPECIES COMPOSITION IN INDUSTRIAL LANDINGS 1979 - 1984

Source: Directorate of Fisheries, Ministry of Commerce and Agriculture

■ Perches   ■ Groupers   ■ Goat fishes   ■ Rabbit fishes   ▨ Shrimps

■ Snappers   ▨ Barracudas   ■ Trevallies   ▨ Grunts   ▨ Other fishes

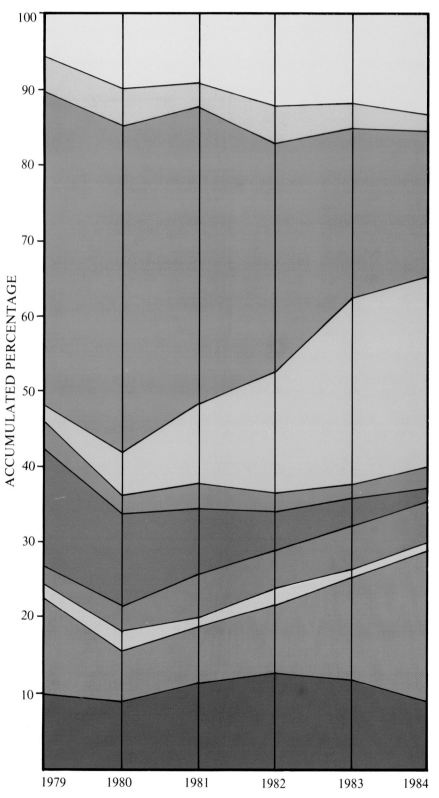

ACCUMULATED PERCENTAGE

1979   1980   1981   1982   1983   1984

Gulf groupers (Vine).

Golden toothless Trevally (Vine).

Table VII : SPECIES COMPOSITION IN ARTISANAL LANDINGS 1979 - 1984

Source: Directorate of Fisheries, Ministry of Commerce and Agriculture

▨ Mackerels	▨ Parrot fishes	▨ Grunts	■ Groupers	▨ Shrimps
▨ Perches	■ Rabbit fishes	■ Snappers	■ Trevallies	☐ Other

Bahrain shrimps (Vine).

Red spot snappers (Vine).

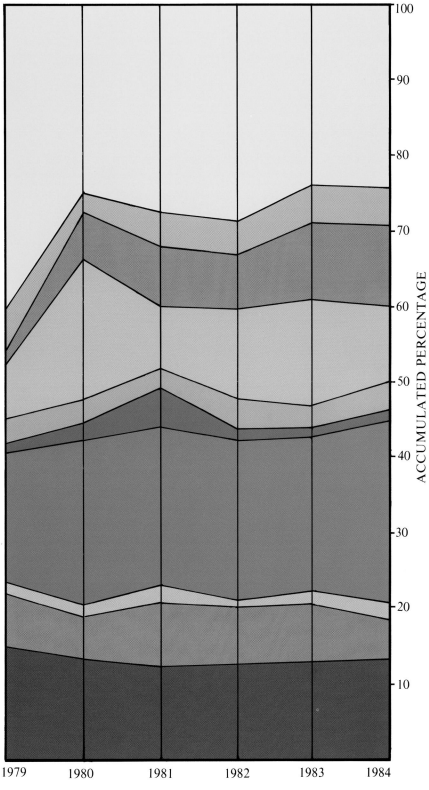

ACCUMULATED PERCENTAGE

1979   1980   1981   1982   1983   1984

Table VIII: Bahrain sea-foods: common, scientific and local names

Trevallies

Seriola sp.	Hamam
Gnathanodon speciosus	Rabeeb (S)
Gnathanodon speciosus	Kefdar (L)
Alepes sp.	Jinees
Trachurus sp.	Khedra
Decapterus sp.	Khedra
Rastrelliger kanagurta	Khedra
Selar crumenophthalmus	Baleg
Seriolina nigrofasciata	Hamam Arabi
Selaroides leptolepis	Seniee

Leather Jackets

Scomberoides commersonianus	Lehlah

Silver Biddies

Gerres oyena	Badeh (L)
Gerres oyena	Musallakh (S)

Perches

Lethrinus lentjan	Sharee
L. miniatus	Soly
L. nebulosus	Soly

Snappers

Lutjanus sanguineus	Hamrah
Lutjanus sp.	Naiser

Mullets

Liza sp.	Maid (S)
Liza sp.	Beyah (L)

Groupers

Epinephelus tauvina	Hamour
E. cf. *jayakari*	Burtam
E. chlorostigma	Summan

Rabbit fishes

Siganus canaliculatus	Saffee
S. javus	S. Senniffee

Mackerels

Scomberomorus commerson	Chana'ad (L)
S. commerson	Khubbat (S)

Tunas

Euthynnus affinis	Jibab
Thunnus abesus	Jibab

Grunts

Plectorhynchus pictus	Khubor
P. schotaf	Janam
P. fangi	Frish

Barracudas

Sphyraena sp.	Jidd (L)
Sphyraena sp.	Dwailmee (S)

Sea breams

Cheimerius sp.	Andag
Mylio cuvieri	Subaity
Rhabdosargus sarba	Gorgofan
Mylio bifasciatus	Faskar
Diplodus kotschyi	Muchawah
Mylio latus	She'em

Goat fishes

Parupeneus sp.	Hamer
Upeneus tragula	Raee
Upeneus sulphureus	Basej

Gar fishes

Tylosuros sp.	Hagool
Ablennes sp.	Hagool
Hemirhamphus far	Sils

Parrot fishes

Scarus sp.	Gain
Choerdon robustus	Gain

Sergeant fishes

Rachycentron canadus	Sikin

Other

Sardinella sp.	O'om
Stelephorus sp.	O'om
Dussumieria sp.	O'om
Pomacanthus maculosus	Anfooz
Formio niger	Imad
Scolopsis ruppellii	Ebzaimee
S. bimaculatus	Ebzaimee
Pelates quadrilineatus	Zamroor
Therapon puta	Zamroor
Platycephalus sp.	Wahar
Pampus argenteus	Zebaidy
Atherina forskalii	Manchos
Chirocentrus sp.	Hiff
Rhonciscus stridens	Jimjam
Istiophorus gladius	Faras
Sillago sp.	Hassom
Dasyatis sp.	Lokhma
Arius thalassinus	Chim
Ariomma indica	Bangara
Saurida sp.	Kassor
Cypselurus sp.	Jaradeh
Nematolosa nasus	Jawaf
Carcharhinus sp.	Jerjoor

Shrimps

Penaeus semisulcatus	Rubian
P. latisulcatus	Rubian
Metapenaeus sp.	Rubian

Crabs

Portunus pelagica	Gubgub

Shovel lobsters

Thennus sp.	Umm Al-Rubian

Cuttle-fish

Sepia sp.	Khathag

Despite the relatively high levels of productivity in the Gulf and its valuable fishery resources, the waters are not as rich in phytoplankton or zooplankton as one might expect. Chlorophyll concentrations in the water column are low (0.49 to 1.28 Mg/ cu.m.) but this contrasts with levels in the sediments which may reach as much as 236 Mg/ cu.m. thus emphasising the importance of benthic productivity. This is further underlined by the presence of huge tracts of sea-grasses *(Halophila ovalis* and *Halodule uninervis)* and benthic algae, sites of primary production which are key factors in the existence of several important species.

Pearl oysters have been fished in the seas around Bahrain for at least four thousand years. Two species of commercial importance, *Pinctada margaritifera* and *Pinctada radiata* are bivalved molluscs living their adult lives on the sea-bed, generally attached by byssus to some hard object. They possess a limited capability to change location by secreting new byssal threads which cling to an adjacent substrate. The oysters feed on diatoms and a range of other plankton such as *Coscinodiscus; Chaetoceros; Trichodesmium; Skeletonema;* larvae of ostracods and even fish eggs. Their diets vary according to what plankton is available at any particular time. Food particles are trapped on the gill filaments and transferred to the labial palps where food is sorted prior to ingestion.

Reproduction of pearl oysters takes place by a process of synchronous spawning. This means that, as a result of some triggering factor, eggs and sperm are ejected into the water where fertilisation takes place and the eggs commence dividing to produce larvae. They have a relatively brief planktonic phase before attaching to some form of substrate. In Bahraini waters many young pearl oysters attach to brown algae. If the alga is dislodged during a storm there is a strong possibility that the juvenile pearl oysters will be cast ashore and thus killed. There are sections of beach on Hawar island where small pearl oyster shells, from a recent recruitment period, can be collected in their tens of thousands — indicating the intense spat settlement which must have occurred and the precarious nature of an oyster's life. The preferred settlement surface of the oyster spat in Bahrain waters seems to be on leaves of the sea-grass *Halodule univervis.* Frequently a single blade may have fifty to a hundred young oysters attached to it and counts of several hundred spat per blade have been made. The main period for settlement is March - April and they grow rapidly during the summer months to a size of around 5mm. During this phase they are an inconspicuous green colour but by October, when the grass blades start to turn brown and die-off, the oysters transfer their grip to an adjacent upright blade. Then as that blade also dries they transfer again. The net result is that large clumps of dark-shelled pearl oysters accumulate and are gradually

transported into deeper water where they form dense aggregations wherever hard substrata are to be found near the base of the sea-grass slopes. This relationship between Bahrain's pearl oysters and the sea-grass beds once again emphasises the vital importance of healthy sea-grass for the maintenance of productive marine-life in the region.

There are several other examples of the vital role played by sea-grasses and the fate of local turtle populations is inextricably linked with healthy sea-grass beds. The Green turtle *(Chelonia mydas)* and the Hawksbill turtle *(Eretomycheles imbricata)* are the two main species of turtle present in Bahrain waters. In addition to these the Leatherback turtle *(Dermochelys coriacea)* and the Loggerhead *(Caretta caretta)* also occur from time to time. Green turtles, the main species present, depend almost entirely on the sea-grass beds for their food. The existence of these feeding grounds has resulted in quite a healthy population of Green turtle residing in the region. They nest on a number of islands between May and September. Shrimp trawl nets prove to be a major hazard and stumbling block in their survival. A co-operative survey of turtle populations was recently instigated by Bahrain and Saudi Arabia in order to assess the turtle populations of the region but it is without doubt that the maintenance of extensive sea-grass beds is a vital factor in their continued existence.

Hawksbill turtle.

The precarious existence of the sea-cow, "Arus el Bahar" otherwise known by its scientific name *Dugong dugon*, also depends almost entirely on these meadows of marine angiosperms. This remarkable creature is the only living herbivorous mammal which is strictly marine and the only surviving species belonging to the family Dugongidae. Its closest relative, Steller's Sea Cow, became extinct about two hundred years ago. Anybody who has had the privilege of seeing dugongs in the wild will be in little doubt about the severe stress which they face or the importance of preserving the last few remaining family groups. Shy, shadowy animals, a fruitful source of fishermans lore, dugongs have been identified with mermaid mythology. However, this sense of mystery has not prevented them from falling prey to fishermen. Their flesh tastes like very tender beef and a single individual may weigh about half a ton, yielding much meat. Feeding mainly on sea-grasses, but also to a much lesser extent on sea-weed, they live in warm waters of the Indo-Pacific region including the Arabian Gulf and the Red Sea.

Despite a wide geographic range, the dugong's habitat requirements are quite specific since they need extensive sea-grasses as a food source and sheltered areas in which to live. Such locations have tended to be more utilised by Man in recent years resulting in considerable disturbance to many of the traditional dugong habitats. The International Union for Conservation of Nature lists the dugong as vulnerable to extinction and it appears that across much of its range it is represented by relict populations separated by large areas of total or partial extinction.

Given this depressing tale of woe it was with little hope of favourable results that the Bahrain-Saudi aerial survey of dugongs began in the autumn of 1985. Helicopters were used to survey large areas of the sea in search of the few wandering dugongs known to exist in the region.

Against everyone's expectations a discovery was made which delighted marine conservationists throughout the world. Following months of finding small numbers of dugongs, suddenly a helicopter search revealed a massive herd of sea-cows. I asked project leader of the survey, Anthony Preen, to tell me what happened. He explained that the dugong herd was located during the first stage (Status Assessment) of Saudi Arabian Meteorological and Environmental Protection Administration's (MEPA's) Dugong Replenishment Project carried out in cooperation with Bahrain's Environment Protection Secretariat. He commented as follows:

"Counts from photographs reveal that the herd, which was remarkably dense, was made up of at least 674 dugongs, about 12 per cent of which were calves. This makes the herd larger than any aggregation of dugongs to have been recorded in the scientific literature.

"What this herd was doing I'm still not sure, but it is becoming apparent that the Gulf waters in which the herd was sighted is a critical habitat of dugongs, especially during winter. In the summer months, with warmer temperatures, they appear to disperse into neighbouring areas although the sighted location probably remains the core-area of their distribution. When we've satellite tracked some dugongs we'll have a better handle on what is happening to them."

Immediately after news of the unique herd's sighting was reported in Bahrain the Government placed a protection order on them. It is to be hoped that these gentle sea-mammals will be left undisturbed and that their numbers will continue to increase. There is no doubt that MEPA's 1986 dugong herd is the most important advance in our knowledge of Indo-Pacific sea-cows to be made for many years.

Opposite and above, left: Aerial views of a large herd of "Arus el Bahar", Dugongs or sea-cows sighted in early 1986 in Bahrain waters (Meteorological and Environmental Protection Administration, Saudi Arabia).

Above right: A close underwater view of dugong on sea-grass bed (Anthony Preen).

Right: Dugong with calf swims over sea-grass bed (Anthony Preen).

Below: A dugong glides to the sea-surface to take a breath of air (Anthony Preen).

While the recorded populations of shrimps, pearl-shells, turtles and dugongs all indicate that the sea-grass beds of Bahrain's shallow coastal waters are far from destroyed, despite the pressures of oil pollution and heavy siltation caused by land-fill and dredging; unfortunately the same cannot be said of another coastal marine plant and creator of a similarly important ecosystem, i.e. the mangrove tree. In times past Bahrain possessed large tracts of healthy mangroves but land reclamation has taken its toll and, despite evidence regarding the importance of the mangroves as high productivity and nursery areas, the vast majority of coastal mangrove systems have been destroyed. However, a valiant attempt is being made to redress the situation and work is underway to replant mangroves in appropriate areas considered suitable for sustaining them. These attempts are meeting with only marginal success but the experiments will be continued and will hopefully yield some useful results in future.

Bahrain's coral-reefs have also suffered as a result of silt accumulation connected with dredging and land-fill operations as well as the deleterious effects on popular reef sites of extensive coral-breakage caused by fishing boat anchors. This is particularly true of reefs along the north-west edge of Fasht Al Adhm close to the east coast of Bahrain. In some ways it is quite surprising that reef-building corals occur at all around Bahrain for, despite the warm sea conditions of summer months, winter sea-temperatures fall significantly below 20 degrees centigrade which is generally considered to be the minimum temperature at which hermatypic corals flourish. In fact, winter sea temperatures fall as low as 13 deg. C. ! In addition, there are considerable salinity fluctuations and, perhaps of greatest significance, regular natural occurrences of high turbidity due to wave disturbance of sediments. Thus, the coral-reefs are already dealing with a number of physical stresses and it may only require a slight deterioration in their conditions for the mortality to occur. We can only marvel at the fact that reef-building corals occur at all in the region and should treasure the delightful reefs which have been created by the relatively few coral species able to exploit the natural marine conditions of the region.

An interesting study on coral associated fish in Bahrain waters by Gregory Smith, Mustafa Saleh and Khatoon Sangoor illustrates the diversity of marine-life found of Bahrain's coral reefs despite the poor growing conditions. Seventy-one species from twenty-five families were recorded from shallow-water reefs (less than 15m deep). A summary of their findings is given in table IX.

Although the diversity is far lower than that occurring on Red Sea reefs it is nevertheless quite high when one takes into account the physico-chemical stresses of the local marine environment. The study also highlights the remarkable high level of

Lutjanus fulviflamma. (Randall).

Cheilodipterus arabicus (Randall).

Plectorhinchus gaterinus. (Randall).

Sea-snake; Hydrophis cyanocinctus. (Randall).

Cuttle-fish; Sepia, *are quite common in the shallow waters around Bahrain and may be found camouflaged over sand during daytime* (Randall).

endemism occurring in the gulf — it lists seven endemics out of the seventy-one recorded species. If one annexes the adjacent zones of the Gulf of Oman and the northwestern Arabian Sea a further five species can be added to the list of endemics bringing the level to 15%. This compares with several other studies of Gulf fauna where a similar degree of endemism has been recorded (eg, Echinoderms 12%; Price, 1982).

Even a brief summary of Bahrain's marine-life, such as this one, would not be complete without mention of those two most feared but generally misunderstood creatures — sea-snakes and sharks. Despite their lethal reputation, sea-snakes are not normally aggressive towards Man. They do however have short venomous grooved fangs near the front of the upper jaw. The following sea-snakes have been recorded in Bahrain waters: — *Enhydrina schitosa, Hydrophis cyanocinctus, Hydrophis lapemoides, Hydrophis ornatus ornatus, Hydrophis spiralis spiralis, Lapemis curtus, Microcephalophis gracilis, Pelamis platurus, Praescutata viperina.*

Fortuately for those skindivers who have come in contact with them sea-snakes have a small gape and

Table IX: Shallow-water reef fishes of Bahrain*

HEMISCYLLIDAE
Chiloscyllium arabicum

PLOTOSIDAE
Plotosus lineatus

SYGNATHIDAE
Doryrhamphus excisus

SERRANIDAE
Cephalopholis hemistiktos
Epinephelus areolatus
E. caeruleopunctatus
E. chlorostigma
E. latifasciatus
E. malabaricus

PSEUDOCHROMIDAE
Pseudochromis dutoiti
P. persicus

APOGONIDAE
Apogon cyanosoma
A. pharaonis
A. taeniatus
Cheilodipterus arabicus
C. quinquelineata
Fowleria variegata

CARANGIDAE
Carangoides ferdau
Gnathanodon speciosus
Selaroides leptolepis

LUTJANIDAE
Lutjanus argentimaculatus
L. ehrenbergi
L. fulviflammus
L. lutjanus
L. russelli

NEMIPTERIDAE
Nemipterus peronii
Scolopsis ghanam
S. taeniatus

HAEMULIDAE
Diagramma pictum
Plectorhinchus gaterinus
P. pictus
P. schotaf
P. sordidus

LETHRINIDAE
Lethrinus elongatus
L. lentjan
L. nebulosus

SPARIDAE
Acanthopagrus berda
A. bifasciatus
Diplodus sargus kotschyi
Sparidentex hasta

MULLIDAE
Parupeneus margaritatus
Upeneus tragula

CHAETODONTIDAE
Chaetodon melapterus
C. nigropunctatus
Heniochus acuminatus

POMACANTHIDAE
Pomacanthus maculosus

POMACENTRIDAE
Abudefduf vaigensis
Amphiprion clarkii
Neopomacentrus sidensis
Pomacentrus aquilus
P. trichourus
Pristotis jerdoni

SPHYRAENIDAE
Sphyraena barracuda

LABRIDAE
Cheilinus lunulatus
Halichoeres stigmaticus
Thalassoma lunare

SCARIDAE
Scarus ghobban
S. persicus
S. sordidus

BLENNIIDAE
Escenius pulcher

GOBIIDAE
Amblygobius albimaculatus
Cryptocentrus lutheri
Istigobius ornatus
Ptereleotris sp.

ACANTHURIDAE
Zebrasoma xanthurum

SIGANIDAE
Siganus canaliculatus
S. javus

OSTRACIIDAE
Ostracion cubicus
O. cyanurus

TETRADONTIDAE
Arothron stellatus
Chelonodon patoca

* from G. Smith (pers. comm.).

therefore experience some difficulty in inflicting an effective bite on humans. Although they are potentially lethal their venom injection usually results in temporary stiffness and muscular pains.

Hydrophis lapemoides is the most common sea-snake in Bahrain waters, possessing a thick body and black head with a pale yellow "v" from the snout to behind each eye. The body has a distinctive pattern of vertical dark brown and yellow bars. The closely related species *Hydrophis cyanocinctus* is very similar to this and is also relatively common in local waters.

It will be of some comfort to the reader to learn that there are no recorded mortalities due to sea-snake bites in the Arabian Gulf.

Sharks of the Arabian Gulf have been recently reviewed by Dr. J. E. Randall in a new book on this topic titled: "Sharks of Arabia", published by IMMEL, 1986.

It is beyond the scope of this book to present a full account of Bahrain's marine-life and the interested reader is referred to more specialised texts dealing with this subject such as Basson et al (1976); Jones (1986) or to the scientific literature on particular groups.

TERRESTRIAL MAMMALS

Having briefly reviewed the terrestrial environment and its flora as well as the marine environment, let us return to the land and consider the mammals which occur on Bahrain. Not surprisingly, the list of species is relatively short since conditions are quite harsh and the islands are not large enough to support great numbers.

As we have already mentioned the main islands of Bahrain were connected to mainland Arabia as recently as seven thousand years ago and had been thus joined for a period of around eighty thousand years. This long-standing land-bridge enabled the islands to be colonised by a range of terrestrial mammals which inhabited mainland Arabia. Today, the islands are cut-off from the mainland and therefore, barring Man's intervention, the mammalian population is isolated from similar species occupying other areas.

In some cases however the isolation of Bahrain's mammalian wildlife has been complete and indigenous strains have developed. The best example of this is perhaps the Cape Hare *(Lepus capensis)* which has morphological and behavioural characteristics distinguishing the Bahrain strain from its mainland relatives. They are extremely attractive, long eared, creatures and noticeably less shy than most hares. The best time to observe them is around dawn or at dusk when they emerge from their temporary hiding places to feed on whatever grasses they can find. During the heat of the day then tend to rest under the shade of trees or bushes.

Some of Bahrain's mammals have probably been replenished from time to time by Man introducing new stock, either deliberately or inadvertently. This applies to the Indian houseshrew *(Suncus murinus)*; Indian grey mongoose *(Herpestes edwardsi)*; gazelle and some rodents. In addition to the hare, those

Opposite: Cape hare (Lepus capensis): *This may be seen especially just before sunset in desert areas and at Al Areen Wildlife Park. When approached it often "freezes" until the last moment.* (Hill).

Above: Long-eared Desert Hedgehog (Paraechinus aetheopicus): *This is a mainly nocturnal insectivore which lives in both desert and cultivated areas. Despite its friendly appearance they may be quite aggressive if cornered and will not hesitate to inflict a painful bite.* (Hill).

Left: Camels. (Hill).

species whose current populations are likely to be the direct result of migrations from Arabia at the time of the ancient land-bridge are the Ethiopian hedgehog *(Paraechinus aethiopicus)* and the Lesser Three-toed Jerboa *(Jaculus jaculus)*.

In order to observe Bahrain's mammals at close quarters a visit to Al Areen Wildlife Park is strongly recommended. My own visit to the park was preceded by a series of telephone calls to its deputy director, Dr. Edgar Allonby. Before receiving permission to visit, my credentials were thoroughly vetted and the timing of my visit was arranged several days in advance. It was only when I arrived there that I fully appreciated the importance of such pre-planning. A special guide has been allocated to me and a vehicle was available for my journey through the park. My guide, Dr. Kate Monk, was carrying out the first study of the behaviour and ecology of gazelle and oryx in wildlife reserves. Her purpose, she explained was to establish the effects of various stocking densities and to establish the biological criteria to support planning strategies for park management of gazelle. Before I set out with Kate Monk, Dr. Allonby briefed me upon

the park's work in the field of wildlife conservation. He explained that much of the original impetus for development of the project had resulted from international action to save the Arabian Oryx from extinction. Two pairs of this species were obtained in 1979 and from these the park had succeeded in building a herd of more than 40 animals by 1986. If the project had achieved nothing else it would have more than justified its existence by thus setting back the clock and re-establishing Bahrain's oryx population.

A consequence of their success in breeding oryx, gazelle, addax and various other species is that the park is rapidly becoming over stocked. A partial solution to this problem is provided by the large fenced reserve adjacent to the park, where small numbers of gazelle or oryx can be released to more or less fend for themselves in a more natural environment.

Wild gazelle do still exist on Bahrain and its islands. During a visit to Hawar island in early 1986 I was once again accompanied by Dr. Kate Monk who was surveying the released populations of gazelle on the main island. In a Landrover search lasting four hours we ranged across the entire island and sighted three groups of gazelle, the largest of which comprised five individuals. They were all Arabian Sand Gazelle *(Gazella subgutterosa marica)* but I was informed that a few Addax had also been recently introduced. The Sand Gazelle is by far the best represented of the locally occurring species. In recent years a herd of approximately 220 has been sighted at Umm Nassan island and it is possible that these are descendants of introductions made by previous rulers. It is known for example that 50 gazelle were introduced here in 1929.

Arabian oryx (Vine)

Opposite: Arabian Sand Gazelle (Gazella subgutterosa
marica): *A timid and fleet-footed desert mammal which roams
in the southern region of Bahrain. It may be seen at Al Areen
Wildlife Park.* (Hill).

Jerboa

Gazella subgutterosa marica is listed in the IUCN Red Data Book as an endangered species in need of complete protection. Bahrain has played an important role in conservation of its population since, apart from the protection afforded by Al Areen, all gazelle in Bahrain have been totally protected by law for some years. The southern section of Bahrain island, Umm Nassan and Hawar island are natural reserves where gazelle experience very little disturbance. A report on gazelle in Bahrain published by the Bahrain Natural History Society in 1984 states that the "wild" population of Bahrain gazelle was as follows:- Bahrain Island — 50-75 Arabian Sand Gazelle or "Reem"; Hawar Island — 15 Arabian Sand Gazelle; Umm Nassan — 200 to 250 of a cross between *Gazella subgutterosa marica* (ie Arabian Sand Gazelle) with *Gazella subgutterosa subgutterosa* plus 11 Blackbuck *(Antilope cervicapra)*.

Studies of wild releases of Arabian Oryx in a number of other countries have revealed a great deal about those resourceful creatures. The desert regions they naturally occupy are so barren that one can do nothing but wonder at their ability to survive. Some answers have stemmed from radio tagging programme on released individuals. These have shown that they may cover enormous distances overnight and can recognise certain land features where water may be found. During the three hottest months of 1983 a group of four oryx released in Oman survived without drinking any water. On a single night this group traversed 60 kilometers of desert and the following night they returned to their original location. Oman's released oryx are now successfully breeding in the wild.

The Lesser Jerboa, a small member of Bahrain's mammalian fauna deserving special mention, is distinguished by a black and white tuft of hair at the end of a long tail; the related Sundevall's *jird* has only a black tuft. Of all the desert creatures jerboas are among the best adapted to survive in the harsh desert conditions which are a feature of their habitat. They can live without water for long periods, creating food stores in their underground burrows and remaining there during particularly hot periods. Captive Jerboas do not drink water since they obtain all their required liquid from their vegetable diet.

AMPHIBIANS AND REPTILES

I was introduced to Bahrain's reptilian fauna while searching for gazelle on Hawar island. We had stopped our Landrover to examine an area of low scrub and marshy ground where vegetation was more abundant than most other places. It appeared to be a likely location for gazelle to rest under the camouflage of the scrub. After walking a few paces from the vehicle I glanced a movement out of the corner of my eye. Looking down at my feet I saw that I had almost trodden on a large spiny tailed lizard *(Uromastyx microlepis)*. It had been standing in the open sunning itself and thus warming its body temperature. I was surprised, first of all by its size. It was almost half a metre in length and had an appearance bordering on that of a prehistoric dinosaur, with a large head born on a long neck and a rotund scaly body lifting high off the ground by its muscular legs. It trailed a broad spiky tail. Instead of fleeing it had turned towards me and was hissing quite aggressively. For a creature of its size it seemed unusually brave. Having gently persuaded our driver that we did not require him to crush it with his foot we managed to coax this magnificent reptile to pose for the camera. The result of that mercurial contre-temps are shown opposite. I learned later that the Spiny Tailed lizard can vary its colour from slate grey to sulphur yellow, usually as a response to rising temperatures. It is a burrowing herbivorous lizard which occasionally supplements its vegetarian diet by taking beetles. My encounter created a lasting impression of a creature which has somehow survived on these islands for many thousands of years and is a living reminder of a prehistoric era. On Bahrain's main island they may be observed in the Central Depression, particularly in the area of the Tree of Life where, on an afternoon walk, one will often discover the lizard in its classic and somewhat determined pose, head raised and front legs extended planted firmly on the ground. *Agama jayakari,* the other Agama lizard occurring here is known locally as "Abu Nufaikh". This species is somewhat smaller than the spiny tailed agama and is easily distinguished since it lacks the broad spiny tail and is differently coloured,

The Fringe Toed Sand Lizard: *Acanthodactylus cantoris schmidti* about 28cms in length, is most

Top: Spiny-tailed Lizard meets biologist on Hawar Island (Vine).

Bottom: Jayakar's Agama Lizard (Agama jayakari): *More common than sightings of it might suggest, this lizard is usually seen on top of small shrubs in the desert or else running across the desert floor. The photo depicts its normal colour phase but when it is alarmed the tail turns bright red and the body becomes a vivid blue.* (Hill).

Common Skink: Common and attractive skink often found in gardens. (Hill).

Below: Bunopus tuberculatus: *A fairly common gecko occuring among buildings and on rocks in semi-desert regions.* (Hill).

Opposite: Persian Gecko (Hemidactylus pericus): *At one time thought to be rare, this gecko is now more commonly found around human habitation.* (Hill).

frequently encountered on loose sand. Its fringed digits enable it to scuttle very rapidly over sand and loose gravel.

The common skink *(Mabuya aurata septemaeniata)* may be found close to cultivated areas of Bahrain but does not occur in the desert. It is familiar to many gardeners.

Geckoes, of which there are at least eight species in Bahrain, rank high among my list of favourite reptiles. They are agile, nocturnal lizards which stalk their insect prey, often in easy view of Man. The yellow-bellied house gecko is a frequent occupant of Bahrain households and a not unwelcome guest. It helps to control the population of house flies, but over and above this utilitarian function, it is difficult not to respond favourably to those large liquid brown eyes staring down from the corner of the ceiling. If captured is is able to shed its tail, a useful escape response from its main bird enemies.

Four snake species have been recorded in Bahrain. Three of these are harmless and one is venomous. The most frequently encountered species is the rat Snake: *Coluber ventromaculatus,* which can exceed one metre in length. It is illustrated on page 67. Although it is not venomous it has sharp teeth and can strike if provoked. It eats small mammals and lizards which it has immobilised by constriction.

The Blind Snake *(Typhlops braminueus)* and Jayakari's Sand Boa are the other two non-venomous species while the Sand snake *(Psammophis schokari)* should be avoided. Despite its common name, it is often found in cultivated areas and can be distinguished by the black line running from the snout, through the eye and along part of the flank. Its general body colour varies from brown to yellowish-grey or olive with a buff streak along the flanks. It is a tree-climber and can grow to around 1.25m. Although theoretically capable of causing severe pain or even death, it is unlikely to inject dangerous quantities of venom. Nevertheless, it should obviously be treated with caution. The other venomous snakes previously mentioned are the sea-snakes.

Among the aquatic reptiles mention should be made of the terrapin *(Clemmys caspica)* which lives in ditches and ponds on the island and the turtles: Green, Loggerhead and Hawksbill, discussed on page 53.

Bahrain's solitary amphibian, the marsh Frog: *Rana ridibunda* lives in ditches, irrigation channels and among reed beds. Tadpoles are found in the spring and early summer.

Opposite, top left: Gecko: Stenodactylus khobarensis *Found on Hawar islands but so far unrecorded from the main island of Bahrain.* (Hill).

Opposite, top right: Gecko: Stenodactylus slevini. *Fairly common and attractive gecko found under debris in desert and semi-desert areas.* (Hill).

Opposite, bottom: Jayakar's Sand Boa (Eryx jayakari): *This attractive sand-boa buries most of its body in sand as a means of camouflaging itself from the small birds which it eats. It leaves its tongue protruding on the surface of the sand in order to attract its prey.* (Hill).

Right: Sand Snake (Psammophis schokari): *Reputedly the only venomous snake in Bahrain; occurs in cultivated areas. Fangs are at back of jaws and it is therefore unlikely to inject much venom into humans.* (Hill).

Below: Rat Snake (Coluber ventromaculatus): *Probably the snake most frequently seen. Inhabits cultivated areas including gardens. Non venomous but aggressive and may bite if provoked.* (Hill).

Right: Terrapin (Clemmys caspica). *This is a fairly common but shy resident of inland freshwater areas.* (Hill).

Below: Marsh Frog (Rana ridibunda): *This is the only species of frog occuring in Bahrain. It is relatively common in drainage ditches and in some ponds.* (Hill).

Opposite: Death's Head Hawkmoth and Caterpillar (Acherontia atropos): *A large hawkmoth with skull-like markings on the back of thorax. Seen from August to May.* (Hill).

INSECTS AND SPIDERS

Bahrain's insect life must be one of the least studied aspects of its natural history. The island does support a rich and varied collection of insects which merit the attention of amateur naturalists and biologists. The setting of a moth trap can help in discovering the great variety of species to be found. Some of the excellent photographs published here are the work of a Bahrain based naturalist. Dr. Mike Hill who has captured many of the hidden wonders of the insect-world so that others may share his own enthusiasm of nature.

One of the few studies concentrating on Bahrain's insect-life dealt with the Lepidoptera (Wiltshire, 1964). Ninety three species were recorded belonging to thirteen families and mention was made of around a dozen species of butterflies, a very low total explained by generally unfavourable climatic conditions.

Left: Preying Mantis: One of several species of preying mantis commonly found on vegetation in Bahrain. It remains immobile until its prey comes within striking distance whereupon it shoots out its powerful front legs and grasps its prey which it proceeds to devour. (Hill).

Below: Oleander Hawkmoth (Daphnis nerii): A large and attractive hawkmoth. Relatively uncommon but may be seen from October to March. (Hill).

Opposite, top: Lime Swallow Tail (Papilio demoleus): *The largest and probably most attractive butterfly of Bahrain. Occurs in cultivated areas from August to April.* (Hill).

Opposite, bottom: Striped Hawkmoth Caterpillar (Celerio livernica): *A brightly coloured caterpillar of Striped Hawkmoth which feeds on the lily-like* Asphodelus tenufolius *which is common in water run-offs following rain in the desert.* (Hill).

Right: Yellow Scorpion: Reputedly more aggressive and venomous than the Black Scorpion which also occurs in Bahrain. (Hill).

Below: Wolf Spider: There are probably several species of wolf spider on the island. All appear to use strength to overpower their victims. They usually live in a hole, often adjacent to a small shrub in the desert. The entrance to their hide-out is made from small twigs bound together with silk threads. (Hill).

BIRD LIFE

We are extremely fortunate that a small but active group of amateur ornithologists have been working for several years on a bird watching programme co-ordinated by the Bahrain Natural History Society. Their own efforts have been aided by short visits from several dedicated bird-watchers who have visited Bahrain purely for the purpose of recording bird migrations or for spotting certain species. From their combined work a clear picture of Bahrain's avian fauna has emerged; more so than of any other aspect of its natural history. The story unfolding is of an island on the migration route of many species and of certain locations within the State which are important breeding sites.

A recent checklist of Bahrain's birds was prepared by Tom Nightingale, an active member of the B.N.H.S. for a number of years. It lists twenty eight species which breed in Bahrain, either as resident breeders, summer visiting breeders or on a casual and opportunistic basis (see table X).

Of special interest to ornithologists are the tumultuous breeding colonies of Socotra cormorants on South Sawad Island in the Hawar group; the Sooty falcons which nest on north-east facing cliffs in the same region and the awe inspiring ospreys whose massive nests form landmarks on some islands. The photographs and captions of Bahrain's bird-life which I am pleased to include in this book tell their own intriguing story of the island's avian fauna and we are indeed indebted to Dr. Mike Hill for this valuable contribution. Readers who would like to delve deeper are recommended to read the fine book by Dr. Hill and Paul Webb — "An Introduction to the Wildlife of Bahrain".

Table X: Checklist of locally breeding birds of Bahrain*

PHALACROCORACIDAE — Cormorants

Socotra Cormorant	*Phalacrocorax nigrogularis*	RB

ARDEIDAE — Bitterns Herons Egrets

Reef Heron	*Egretta gularis*	RB

PANDIONIDAE —Osprey

Osprey	*Pandion haliaetus*	RB

FALCONIDAE— Falcons

Sooty Falcon	*Falco concolor*	SVB

RALLIDAE — Rails Crakes

Moorhen	*Gallinula chloropus*	RB

CHARADRIIDAE — Plovers

Kentish Plover	*Charadrius alexandrinus*	RB

STERNIDAE — Terns

Caspian Tern	*Sterna caspia*	RB
White-cheeked Tern	*Sterna repressa*	SVB
Bridled Tern	*Sterna anaethetus*	SVB
Saunders Little Tern	*Sterna saundersi*	SVB

COLUMBIDAE — Pigeons Doves

Collared Dove	*Streptopelia decaocto*	RB
Turtle Dove	*Streptopelia turtur*	SVB

PSITTACIDAE — Parrots etc.

Rose-ringed Parakeet	*Psittacula krameri*	RB

TYTONIDAE — Barn Owls

Barn Owl	*Tyto alba*	RB

APODIDAE — Swifts

Pallid Swift	*Apus pallidus*	RB

UPUPIDAE — Hoopoes

Hoopoe	*Upupa epops*	CB

ALAUDIDAE — Larks

Black-crowned Finch Lark	*Eremopterix nigriceps*	RB
Desert Lark	*Ammomanes deserti*	RB
Hoopoe Lark	*Alaemon alaudipes*	RB
Crested Lark	*Galerida cristata*	RB

HIRUNDINIDAE — Swallows Martins

Swallow	*Hirundo rustica*	CB

PYCNONOTIDAE — Bulbuls

White-cheeked Bulbul	*Pycnonotus leucogenys*	RB

TURDIDAE — Chats Thrushes

Rufous Bushchat	*Cercotrichas galactotes*	SVB

SYLVIIDAE — Old World Warblers

Graceful Warbler	*Prinia gracilis*	RB
Olivaceous Warbler	*Hippolais pallida*	SVB

LANIIDAE — Shrikes

Great Grey Shrike	*Lanius excubitor*	RB

CORVIDAE — Crows etc.

Indian House Crow	*Corvus splendens*	CB

PASSERIDAE — Sparrows

House Sparrow	*Passer domesticus*	RB

The key to abbreviations used

CB = *Casual Breeder* : Isolated opportunistic breeding has occurred.

RB = *Resident Breeder* : Present throughout the year and breeding.

SVB = *Summer Visitor Breeding* : Self Explanatory.

* after Tom Nightingale, Bahrain Natural History Society Report, 1983.

Opposite: Grey Heron — Bahrain, (Ardea cinerea): Despite the absence of any evidence that it breeds locally, birds are present throughout the year (Hill).

Left: Socotra Cormorant — immature, Hawar Islands. (Hill).

Above: Socotra Cormorant colony — Hawar Islands. (Phalacrocora nigrogolaris): *A large colony of up to 250,000 birds nests on one of the Hawar Islands during October to January period.* (Hill).

Below: Socotra Cormorant at nest. Hawar Islands: The nest is a circular indentation in the ground. Nests tend to be arranged in groups of about 50 within the colony. 2 to 4 eggs are laid. (Hill).

Left: Turnstone (Arenaria interpres). (Hill).

Below: Greater Flamingoes — Bahrain, Tubli Bay (Phoenicopterus ruber): *Up to eighty of these colourful and elegant birds are to be found in the coastal areas of Bahrain throughout the year. There is no evidence of breeding.* (Hill).

Opposite, top: Common Sandpiper (Actitis hypoleucos): *An active wader usually seen singly in ditches, near freshwater and occasionally on the shoreline; throughout the year.* (Hill).

Opposite, bottom: Curlew Sandpipers (Calidris ferruginea) — *Bahrain: Large numbers of this active wader are seen on the mudflats around Bahrain during the autumn migration.* (Hill).

Opposite, top left: Yellow Wagtail (Motacilla flava): *A fairly common passage migrant, especially during spring. A number of races occur here. This is the blue-headed variety. Often appear in large flocks.* (Hill).

Opposite, top right: European Roller (Coracias garrulus): *This is an attractive and regular migrant visitor to Bahrain during spring and autumn.* (Hill).

Opposite, bottom: European Bee-Eater (Merops apiaster): *This most colourful bird may be seen in flocks during its migration time, especially during March - April. Sometimes large numbers pass over an area, catching insects on the wing, and issuing a fluty call.* (Hill).

Right: Hoopoe (Upupa epops): *Although seen at all times of year in small numbers there is an upsurge of numbers during the passage times. It is probably the most distinctive migrant to occur on Bahrain and may be observed in both desert areas and among residential gardens.* (Hill).

Below: Little Egret — Bahrain, (Egretta garzetta): *Essentially a winter visitor to Bahrain, where it may be seen in quite large numbers, usually but not only along the shoreline. Evening roosts around Adhari in wintertime may have fifty or more birds in a single tree.* (Hill).

Slender billed gulls at sunset — Tubli bay, Bahrain (Larus genei). (Hill).

CONSERVATION

The reader will by now realise that there is plenty to learn about Bahrain's natural history. Conservation of the island's wildlife has been of concern to the Government of Bahrain for many years. The project at Al Areen has made an important contribution towards re-establishing certain species. The Environmental Protection Secretariat has concentrated many of its efforts on the marine environment where large development projects have taken place. Not all of these have a harmful effect on sea-life. The Bahrain-Saudi causeway, for example, has had several beneficial results such as increasing the scour effect by concentrating water flow and it has introduced a large new surface area of hard substrate into a region where many sessile invertebrates experience difficulty in locating suitable settlement surfaces.

Efforts have been made to reverse the damage done to some habitats and the concept of environmental enhancement has led to projects such as replanting of mangroves and attempts to create new productive coral-reefs by building artificial reefs. Scientists have continually emphasised the importance of critical habitats whether these have been marine, coastal or terrestrial and the Bahrain Government has been quick to respond to many conservation issues. Equally, scientists have learned that it is possible to minimise the damage caused by development projects providing they are able to study the situation before work commences and to make recommendations which are carried out by the developer. As we shall see in subsequent sections of this book Bahrain has preserved a great deal of its cultural heritage while forging ahead with modern development on a grand scale. The country's wild-life could hardly remain unaffected by such rapid and intense activity as has occurred over the last thirty or so years but it is good to report that not all of the effects have been for the worse. Continued vigilance and sustained efforts should result in the preservation of Bahrain's rich natural heritage for the enjoyment and appreciation of future generations.

Below: Cloth weaving at Bani Jamra (Vine)

Right: At the races. (Vine).

Opposite, top: Young eyes. (Pradhan).

Opposite, bottom: Traditional dress and locally produced jewellery grace the fine features of a Bahraini girl. (Directorate of Cultural Heritage).

TRADITIONS

To forget ones origins and the archaeological, geological, cultural and historical dimensions that have gone between, is to forego a deep personal awareness which underlies stability and continuity in society.

Bahrain owes a great deal to its vigorous traditions. Beneath the veneer of twentieth century modernity lies this alluring changeless facet, continuously bewitching all those who come in contact with it.

The people of Bahrain, warm, generous, hospitable, relaxed and confident contribute enormously in making the country a very special place. The strength of character and forceful personality found in so many Bahrainis is undoubtedly the result of adherence to long-standing traditions and, as we have seen, a considerable degree of continuity from generation to generation. Modern life can ride rough shod over treasured and venerable customs so undermining the very fabric of a nation's culture build up over centuries. However, the intrinsic value of ancestral traditions, ancient crafts and ethnic customs is gaining recognition by a growing band of devoted enthusiasts who are playing an important role in preserving national traditions and accompanying social values.

Visitors interested to learn more about local traditions and cultural heritage are strongly recommended to pay a visit to Bahrain National Museum and the Cultural Heritage Centre where a series of displays portray many fascinating aspects of the State's inheritance including ancient artefacts; traditional dress; falconry; pearl diving and boat

building. If time is available the discerning traveller should delve deeper and visit the actual sites of historic or cultural interest. Such an excursion, or more likely a series of excursions, is well worth the effort and can be arranged by one of several tour operators. "Bahrain Explored" guided me on several interesting visits. It is the longest established company specialising in island tours with knowledgable and experienced guides specialising in ancient history and sites of photogenic interest. Alternatively, one can use the excellent route plans provided in Angela Clarke's book: "The Islands of Bahrain" or in several tourist maps.

'Where are the pearl divers?', is one of the first questions many visitors ask. Bahrain is justly famous for its pearls and it is still possible to find specialised pearl dealers and some very fine pearl jewellery in the souks of Manama and Muharraq. The pearl-fishing beds surrounding Bahrain are among the best in the World but commercial pearl fishing has more or less died-out, a consequence of a fall in pearl prices following the Japanese development of pearl culture techniques. This has been compounded by a tendency for Bahrainis to work in the oil industry or other land-based jobs rather than to accept the dangers and insecurity of pearl diving. This is entirely understandable and nobody would wish for the hardships of those earlier pearl diving days to be revived. It is nevertheless true that a rich natural resource in the form of extensive pearl oyster beds has remained relatively unexploited for the last few decades. Current investigations by scientists working with the Environmental Protection Secretariat are seeking to establish the prospects for a renewal of the

Above: This graphic reconstruction of life aboard a pearling vessel may be seen at Bahrain's Heritage Centre. (Vine).

Left: The pearl-fishing exhibition at Bahrain's Heritage Centre comprises several excellent models of the craft and equipment used by Bahraini pearl divers. (Vine).

Pearl divers. (Falcon).

pearl oyster industry in Bahraini waters. If this should happen elderly and retired pearl-divers will be well pleased that their traditions will not totally disappear.

Much folk-lore accompanied pearl diving and none reflects the romanticism of pearl-divers more than their unique music. As the vessels approached the pearl banks and divers readied themselves for their various tasks, a naha'an (professional singer) especially selected by the captain, would strike-up and the sailors all joined in as they continued to work. Each song had a rhythm to suit a particular task and, like sea-shanties of western sailors, the music became an inspiration for good team-work. The origins of this music are lost in time but it seems most likely that it evolved through generations of Bahraini pearl divers influenced by Indian and perhaps African music. The 'Snguini', 'Khatfa' and 'Dhowaria' comprise the three categories into which this folk-music falls. The first of these (the 'Sanguinia') was sung during the launching ceremony of new pearling dhows. It is haunting, rhythmic music befitting the seriousness of the occasion. As divers heave the ropes to haul their newly born dhow into the sea, their song tells of the boat's construction, its fragility in the face of storms and the uncertain future which it faces. The second type of song, the 'Khafta' is quite different. It is cheerful music played with the accompaniment of finger cymbals and a bass drum, and sung by divers enroute to the pearl-banks in generally happy mood as they sailed their vessel, heaved on the halliards, and adjusted their sails to catch each breath of wind.

Opposite, top: Bahrain's natural pearls are regarded as the finest in the World (Falcon).

Opposite, bottom: Pearl jewellery. (Vine).

Right: Pearl divers. (Falcon).

The pearling vessels selected a postion on the pearl banks and dropped their heavy anchors. As the warps were passed out and the real task was about to commence, divers chanted the 'Dhowaria'. Once the moorings were firmly in place diving could commence. In his account of life in Bahrain during the early part of this century, the late Sir Charles Belgrave described several visits he made to the extremely active pearl diving fleet of that period. Indeed, a great deal of Bahrain's wealth depended upon the results of the pearling season. If it had been successful money from the diving crews, boat owners and pearl merchants circulated in the bazaar, the ensuing benefits being felt by the entire community. The Government did not tax the pearl divers or pearling merchants but the wealth created by fruitful pearl harvests led to an increase in imports and consequent customs revenues. In the early 1900's there were still around 20,000 men employed in the industry during the pearling season. The departure of the fleet was an enthralling sight which could not fail to move either the participants or those left behind on shore. Belgrave writes of his first such experience as follows:—

"I shall never forget the first time I saw the pearling fleet set out from Muharraq. It was evening and the tide was full. The graceful ships, like Roman galleys, with huge lateen sails, moved smoothly through the irridescent water, silhouetted against the sunset sky. The sound of sailors singing and the throbbing of their drums was borne across the water to where I stood with the people who were watching the departure."

Already, however, engines were being used by a few vessels and Belgrave recognised that he would probably not be able to observe such a traditional spectacle for many more years. He was right, but for the wrong reason. At that time cultured pearls were not threatening the market but it was not long before the effects of this burgeoning industry led to a decline in the market for natural pearls.

In 1926 Charles Belgrave made his first visit to the pearling fleet working offshore. He describes this experience in his book "Personal Column":—

"I clambered up the slippery side of the dhow on a loose rope and was received by the captain, who invited me to join him on a sort of shelf in the poop where he slept and kept his carved wooden sea-chest, which contained his own belongings and the pearls. The crew, who numbered about sixty men, were squatting in the middle of the deck around a huge heap of shells which had been caught the previous day. With their short knives they prised open every shell, searching each one carefully, prodding about in the flesh of the oyster. When a man found a pearl he placed it between his toes and when two or three were collected he handed them over to the captain who watched the men from his eyrie with an eagle eye. . . ."

On this occasion Belgrave asked the divers whether they knew how pearls are made. They answered with one of the folkloric myths which must have been passed from generation to generation of diver. They explained to him that when it rains the pearl oysters swim to the surface of the sea, open their shells and receive a drop of rain-water. It was these which later became pearls! We now know, of course, that the true stimulus for oysters to form pearls comes from a grain of sand or other small fragment lodged in the mantle. The oyster secretes its shining nacreous layers around this in the same way that it deposits pearly nacre around the inner surfaces of the shell valves. It is possible that conditions of high turbidity brought about by wave action dictates the relatively high incidence of pearls in *Pinctada margaritifera* collected from Bahrain waters. Not all pearl shell populations occur where the sea becomes so regularly disturbed. In the clear waters of the Red Sea for example, pearl oysters of Dunganab bay have a very low incidence of natural pearls.

Bahraini fishermen developed their own pearl-diving techniques which, while being extremely labour intensive, did bear fruit. The divers worked in tandem with "pullers" who were responsible for heaving up the baskets of pearl shells.

In order to select an exact location on the pearl-banks the vessels were rowed:—

"After a long discussion between the captain, his mate, and some of the divers, it was decided where the day's diving would begin, and the anchor was hauled up. Everything on board the dhow was done to the accompaniment of singing, stamping and hand-clapping, especially when the men were at the oars. As they heaved the square bladed oars through the water, keeping excellent time, their voices rose and then descended in a sound like a long drawn-out groan, but many of their diving songs were lively and tuneful . . ."

Belgrave commented that once the vessel had reached its chosen location the oars were lashed to the rowlocks so that they projected over the water and diving commenced. A diver increased the speed of his descent by placing his feet into the loop of a weighted rope as it was lowered to the sea-bed. He then placed as many shells as he could grab in about a minute into a bag clutched tightly during his descent. A sharp tug signalled to his "puller" to heave both him and the oyster bag back upto the surface. Dives were usually made to around ten or eleven metres but they were capable of fishing the deeper banks around twenty to twenty five metres deep.

There was a definite rhythm to this activity which must have had a number of advantages in terms of monitoring the divers' work, checking on their safety and logging the productivity of a particular oyster bank. The divers all descended together and, after each dive they waited on the surface until all had

emerged whereupon the pullers ("Saibs") carried out their part of the "dance" — to the accompaniment of a rhythmic chant they carried the full bags to the central heap on deck and all emptied them in unison. This would be repeated for ten dives, after which the divers came back on board to rest and warm-up with a cup of coffee while their place was taken by a second relay of divers so there was no break in the work.

Pearling had been practised around Bahrain, on a continuous basis, for approximately four thousand years. At the beginning of this century there were around 900 vessels engaged in pearl fishing based out of Bahrain and about half the island's male population were working in the pearl business. In 1909 the pearl harvest was worth a million pounds sterling and it seemed that nothing could happen to break such a long established natural industry. The depression encompassing Europe in the 1920's caused a sudden drop in demand however and then, in 1932, the cultured pearl market started to expand. 1945 witnessed the last vigorous attempts at rejuvenating the dying pearl fishing industry. In the following years fewer and fewer vessels sailed to the pearl banks and the traditions of Bahrain pearl fishing, passed on from

generation to generation for literally thousands of years, slowly expired.

Despite the decline of the pearling industry Bahrain is still renowned for its pearl merchants, pearl jewellery and the high quality of its natural pearls. It is possible that a means will be found to revive some aspects of this ancient activity.

Bahrain's renowned pearling industry was part of its overall fishing and maritime activities. Boats which had carried pearl divers to the banks during summer months often reverted to catching fish in cooler periods. The fishing vessels were built in Bahrain by craftsmen whose art was based upon a long history of boat-building centred on construction by eye rather that the use of any written plans. It is still possible to see such craft being built by these traditional methods in Bahrain. Piles of uncut tree-trunks and snaking branches imported from India totter outside the boat yards to be selected and hewn into the ribs of vessels by the master boat builders. Carpenters still rely mainly on a few hand-tools including hammer, saw, adze, chisel, plane and caulking iron. To these have been added the sophistication of electric drill and electric sanding machines.

The large ocean going "Boum" and its smaller version, the "Sambuk" (used for pearl-diving); the "Shu'i" (up to 50m) and the "Jalbut" (distinguished by its vertical stem) comprise the major categories of vessel still used in Bahrain. The Boum is a double ended craft still retaining its hull-shape from the pre-Portuguese era. It seems likely that the design originated in Bahrain and spread to other areas such as Oman. This is the largest of the extant Arabian wooden sailing vessels with tonnage reaching 400 tons and dimensions of 50 to 120 feet in length and 15 to 30 feet in width. The design is characterised by a long straight planked bow-sprit, angled at about 45 degrees.

The Sambuk (or Sambuq) possesses a low finely tapered bow and a high transom stern. It is one of the most graceful and evocative of Arabian vessels and has been widely used throughout the Gulf, Arabian coast and the Red Sea although there are regional variations in overall size and dimensions. Sambuks are today used as general purpose fishing and trading vessels but they were previously favoured for pearling.

The Shu'i is a small version of a Sambuk, not exceeding 15 tons, and has a straight, rather than a curved, stem piece.

The derivation of the Sambuk/Shu'i design is almost certainly from Portuguese caravels which penetrated these waters early in the sixteenth century. There is little doubt that Bahraini boat builders, along with other Arabian shipwrights, were impressed by the seaworthiness and sailing characteristics of the caravels. Their design was adapted over the years to local sailing conditions.

The Jalibut on the other hand seems to be derived from an English Naval Jollyboat. It is more launch shaped than any of the other designs and is characterised by a straight vertical bow. They were also used for pearling but they lack the fine, seaworthy lines of the Sambuk or Boum.

I was introduced to traditional techniques of boat building at the Manama dhow building area, just a few minutes walk from the heart of the modern city and its diplomatic enclave. A row of wooden sheds lie adjacent to a vast expanse of flat, reclaimed land. The coastline may have shifted a few hundred metres but the boat builders have stayed right where they have lived for hundreds of years. Their rickety-roofed sheds and rush fencing compounds house some huge wooden dhows being built by methods which have hardly changed for four centuries. A short walk along the line of sheds revealed Sambuks and Shu'i in various stages of completion demonstrating methods of construction better than any text book could hope to explain. The master builders were extremely hospitable, welcoming me to inspect their work and allowing me to clamber up ladders to view the vessels' interiors.

A constant source of wonderment to the western observer, the craft are built by a procedure which is basically the reverse of that employed by European boatbuilders. Instead of first constructing a framework of ribs to which the planks are nailed, local builders construct a shell of planks to which the ribs are fitted in sections. The method is almost certainly derived from the earlier system of sewing planks together. Vessels are made by carvel construction; i.e. planks are laid flush to each other. Although the building is done by eye, templates are used to check on the shape of the planking at various points along the length of the boat. While planking is usually of teak imported from India, the ribs are made

Below: Fishing vessels at Manama. (Vine)

*Opposite: Boat-building at Manama's dhow construction area,
The method of construction is the reverse of the European
method in that ribs are fitted, after the planks have been shaped.*
(Vine).

from trees known as "mit" brought from Iraq, India
or Somalia. Indeed, virtually all the wood for
Bahrain's long established boat building industry is
imported, underlining the entrepôt role Bahrain
played in Gulf trade since the dawn of history. Trade
links between Bahrain, India and Iraq have been
established for four or five thousand years. It is little
wonder therefore that Bahrain's boat builders are so
familiar with the various types of timber derived from
these distant lands.

I was fortunate to arrive at a time when a large
vessel was at the first stage of its construction. The
keel had been laid and stem and stern posts fitted. The
boat-builders, having laid the garboard strakes, were
engaged in fixing the planks, starting with those on
each side of the keel and working up towards the
water-line. The planks are physically bent into the
desired form, and in order to maintain their shape
temporary templates are fixed to the outside of the
planks. These constructional aids are removed once
the inner frame-work of ribs and strakes has been
fitted into the hull.

In the adjacent shed a little more progress had been
achieved on a similar vessel. The keelson was fitted

and a series of floor timbers had been firmly attached
to the keel. Some of these were already scarf joined to
sturdy ribs or futtocks extending as far as the
gunwhale. Horizontal stringers had been nailed to the
ribs and planking had already reached the water-line
level of the hull. As I watched one of the builders, in
about the only concessions to modern machinery
which I noted, used an electric drill to bore holes in
the planks through which oiled nails are later driven.
On climbing the wooden ladder lying next to the
massive timber hull I was able to see that the
shipwrights had laid deck beams across the top of the
hull, resting on broad stringers reinforced with knees.
I was told that once the hull was ready it would be
caulked with a mixture of raw cotton soaked in
coconut oil or shark-liver oil. One recently completed
vessel had been painted with shark-liver oil giving it a
rich, shiny varnished appearance.

Around the turn of the century Bahrain had a
reputation throughout the Gulf for producing the
finest quality cotton sail-cloth, hand woven by the
cloth weavers of Bani Jamra. The sails were carefully
cut to have just the desired amount of bag when they
were correctly set. Unfortunately, the advent of low-

Gargoor fish-traps under various stages of construction. These are the most important fishing equipment in use, contributing 40.5% of the industrial fish catch in 1984. (Vine).

cost fuel has meant that many boums are now completely motorised and dependence on sail-power has been retained by very few vessels.

Little more than a stone's throw from the boat-building sheds are a number of spacious open wooden buildings where craftsmen weave long strands of wire into beautifully shaped "Duwabi" fish traps. Having many times seen the traps piled high on the decks of fishing boats, or underwater, set on the reefs, I had always assumed that they were built from prefabricated sheets of wire netting rather than being individually woven from long strands of strong wire. It is a truly fascinating sight to watch these trap makers at work. The floor of the sheds are covered by soft sand which helps to hold the wires in place when they are laid out, at the initial phase of each trap's construction. To begin, a patch of sand is patted into a circular depression into which are carefully arranged radiating strands to form the upright frame of the mesh-work. Wires snake out in long lines across the floor of the shed and then out and across the adjacent reclaimed land. In each shed there are about eight or ten traps in the making and the floors are criss-crossed by multiple strands of thin wire. As the trap sides begin to take shape the weaver gradually

cages himself in working from within the structure, at first sitting cross-legged, then crouching, and finally standing as he swivels around the cage flicking the wires in and out with such nonchalant dexterity that it is difficult to capture the full technique by eye. Upon reaching the top of the trap the weaver leaves a gap through which he is able to extricate himself, and which he later finishes off to form the entrance collar.

Unfortunately, if these large traps are left unattended on the sea-bed, perhaps as a result of a marker float becoming detached, they continue to lure fish for a very long period. It is not unusual to discover abandoned traps on the sea-bed, containing many fish. In some cases these can include a grouper which devours smaller fish entering the trap. Some fish die of starvation in these watery graves — an unfortunate waste of a valuable resource.

Looking across towards Halat As-Sulatah from the shore-line at Hidd where hadra fish-traps are fished daily at low-tide. (Vine).

There is another kind of traditional fish-trap in use around the shallow-waters of Bahrain. This is the fixed "Hadra" trap which is generally constructed from palm branches held together by rope. The traps straddle inter-tidal and shallow sub-tidal zones and are laid so that fish moving along the shore, as the tide ebbs, are lured along the long wall or "yad" towards deeper water. At the seaward end of the yad the walls curve around forming a trap or "hawsh" from which the fish are unable to escape. They remain within it, in a deepened enclosure, the "sirr", until the fishermen arrive at low tide, shouldering their matting baskets, small nets and fish spears in order to extricate their catch. Certain locations are much better than others for this type of fixed trap and a great deal of folklore has built up around traditional family rights to particular sites. Each trap is known by a particular name, duly registered with the authorities, and the rights over a trap are closely guarded. In 1934 there were 868 hadra along the northern shores of Bahrain. Since then many traps have been abandoned or destroyed by land reclamation. There are however still numerous working examples to be seen around the coast. Not all of them are operated by their owners since, in some cases, they are rented out to fishermen for a cash payment.

Basket-makers use palm-leaves and natural-dyes to weave baskets in the traditional manner. (Vine).

The traditional crafts of Bahrain are based upon relatively few locally occuring raw materials. Thus, for example, rush matting is woven from a grass growing along the boundary between more saline coastal soils and those irrigated by spring-water. The mats, made by Sitra craftsmen, are well used in Mosques and houses throughout Bahrain. Basketwork utilises dried palm leaves generally collected from the weaver's immediate surroundings since they are to be found working in the midst of palm groves, in small barasti enclosures. Pottery workers at Aali use clay from the hills around Rifaa and their kilns are often built from four thousand year old tombs! They make a useful range of incense bowls, water jugs and drinking cups and in doing so are maintaining a local tradition which has existed for several millenia! Lime is manufactured from local stone and fires in the same kilns as those used by the potters. Gypsum, as we have already noted, occurs locally in large deposits, just beneath the soil surface, on many parts of the island. Slabs are quarried and fired in a similar manner to lime. When mixed with water it forms a quick setting cement used as lining for some ancient tumuli and is still favoured today for making ceiling and wall decorations.

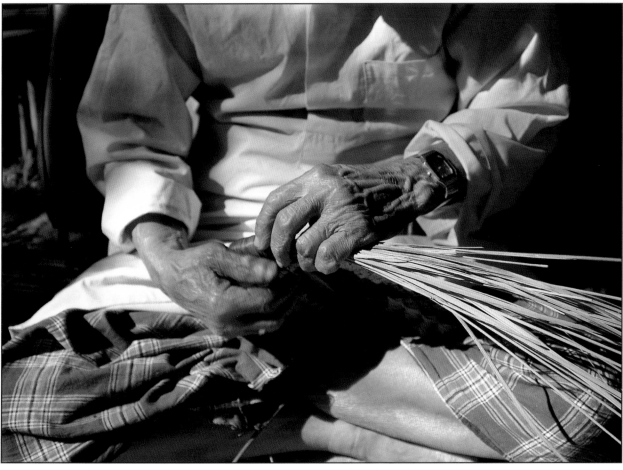

Right: Practicing a craft almost as old as Bahrain itself, a potter uses a short length of string to mould the pot spinning on his wheel. (Directorate of Heritage and Museums).

Below: Raising the temperature of a potter's kiln. (Pradhan).

Pottery at Aali village. (Vine).

Cloth weaving at Bani Jamra (Vine).

The cloth weavers of Bani Jamra are, alas, a declining breed. Their work requires long hours and considerable dedication, inevitably straining eyes and back muscles. There are however still several skilled weavers in the village and its environs. Their products are presently gaining a special rarity value. Abdullah is an elderly, gentle and charming cloth weaver whom I visited one March afternoon with Elsa Cook from "Bahrain Explored". Elsa and Abdullah greeted each other like long lost friends and they spent several minutes discussing their various families and each other's health before Abdullah recommenced his work. He sat on the ground behind the loom, his feet in a trench excavated to house the peddles. In front of him, on the hot sand, the threads to be woven into a brightly coloured "awzar" were arranged in long parallel lengths. As he continued to chat with Elsa he paddled the loom while shooting the weft back and forth, each time selecting the colour of thread required to form the desired pattern. For Abdullah, our arrival was more of a diversion than an intrusion and we were both made to feel genuinely welcome. In addition to being impressed by the quality of the cloth he wove on such a rudimentary loom, I was deeply moved by his serenity and warm hospitality. Apart from the "awzar" (a wrap-around skirt) which we saw on the loom, Abdullah also makes the traditional black garment used by Bahraini women, the "abba". Some completed ones were folded on a pole behind him. Several had gold thread interwoven, creating a rich contrast against the black cloth. This embellishment of the abba with gold-thread is a practice which has been carried out for some time. Writing of his experience during the 1920's, the late Sir Charles Belgrave commented as follows:—

"Ladies of the upper classes had their abbas edged with gold thread and decorated with big gold tassles. When the "abbas" wore out, the gold thread survived and hawkers used to go through the streets in the mornings singing 'zerri atiq; zerri atiq' (old gold thread) which they bought from the women at the house doors. They refurbished it and sold it to the makers of the abbas."

Interior decorations of a pearl merchant's house, Muharraq. (Morris).

Traditional carpentry in the form of carved doors, lattice panels ("moushribiyas") or furniture is still made by hand at Alawi Furniture Works. Copper coffee pots are increasingly harder to find since most metal-smiths only work in tin and pure copper-smiths are very few in number. It is however, still possible to locate examples in local antique shops if one persists in one's search. Embroidery is yet another craft which flourishes. Women of several villages, including Busaibi and Sanabis, embroider intricate patterns onto their national costumes and these are then sold in the Wednesday Market. Gold embroidery is also sewn into the formal woolen clothes worn by Bahraini men on special occasions.

(Directorate of Heritage and Museums).

At Bahrain's magnificent race-course ancient traditions merge gracefully with upto the minute progress. A manicured green track provides a near perfect running surface for pure-bred Arabian horses ridden by silk-clad jockeys. Spectators follow the events from the comfort of a gigantic stand in the shape of a bedouin tend. Racing enthusiasts come here for the sheer fun of the racing and not to bet since gambling is prohibited. The highly valued pure bred Arabian horse partly originates from Bahraini bloodstock. Horses sent from Bahrain as gifts from Shaikh Mohammed al-Khalifa to Abbas Pasha of Egypt in the middle of the last century helped to establish an Egyptian Arabian stud. One famous mare called "Bint al-Bahrain" was presented by Shaikh Isa Bin Ali (great grandfather of the present Emir) to the Khedive of Egypt. These horses formed part of a nucleus of Arabian stock which were used to establish a "pure-bred" line. A visit to Bahrain race-course provides a wonderful opportunity to observe the finest quality of Bahrain Arabian horses at close quarters. These are beautiful streamlined and remarkably compact creatures standing at around 15 hands high. A deep girth and muscular thighs contribute to the power and strength of the animal so that even the simplest movement is conducted with spirit and energy. A perfect topline and tail carriage, coupled with lively eyes set in a noble head add grace and beauty to each stride. The colour varies from dark to grey or chestnut with the most typical form being a dark bay with black points.

There are around twenty different strains of Bahrain Arabian horses currently bred on the island. The strongest stallion strains are drawn from the oldest lines such as Kuheilan, Jallaby and Dahman. There is no doubt that the horse has a special place in the hearts of all Bahrainis. Historically, speed, manouverability and intelligence gave the rider a better chance of survival in battle. Nowadays, even though they have become redundant in conflict and for transport purposes, the animal is still greatly admired and appreciated for its sheer beauty and fine sporting qualities. The Al-Khalifa were always great horse lovers and none more so than the present Amir, Shaikh Isa, who has done so much to foster the breeding of Arabian race-horses on Bahrain.

In addition to horses and camels, the Saluki dog and hunting falcons (particularly the Saker and peregrine) have also played an important role in the lives of Bahrainis.

The traditional quarry of Bahrain's falconers is the Houbara otherwise known as Macqueen's Bustard (*Chlamydotis undulata macqueenii*). It is one of the smaller members of the Bustard family, weighing around 2.5kg. as opposed to the much larger Great Bustard which often exceeds 10kgs. Unfortunately Houbara are becoming increasingly rare. They are in any case extremely shy birds favouring remote uninhabited semi-desert regions. When hunted by falcons they avoid discovery by lying flat and motionless on the sand with neck outstretched. In such a "frozen" posture falcons have difficulty in recognising them but once they move there is an immediate "battle of wits" between the fast flying Houbara and the lethally efficient hunting falcon.

Houbara migrate towards the southern deserts of the Arabian peninsula, passing through Bahrain in November or early December. they return northwards again in March. Featuring strongly in the folklore of Arabia, there have been a number of attempts to establish breeding populations of this species and to thus revive its dwindling numbers. One such project may be seen at Al Areen Wildlife Park.

Below: Falconing has been practiced in Bahrain for many centuries. Using mostly Peregrine and Saker's Falcons the traditional quarry is Hubara Bustard a species whose numbers have declined in recent years. (Directorate of Heritage and Museums).

With a turn of speed of 65 kilometers per hour, the Saluki is capable of out-running even the most sprightly gazelle. Their recorded history precedes that of any other dog breed since paintings of them have been discovered on 7,000 year old pottery and on Anatolian wall paintings around six thousand years old. Bahraini Salukis belong to the feathered coat variety but are somewhat larger than those living elsewhere. Regarded as "royal dogs", in recent years the pure-bred royal pack had been revived by Dana al-Khalifa who was originally presented with two pure-bred puppies by Shaikh Khalifa Bin Sulman al Khalifa. The strain's purity is certified by the U.K. Kennel Club which expects the following appearance:

". . . should give an impression of grace and symmetry and of great speed and endurance, coupled with strength and activity to enable it to kill a gazelle or other quarry over deep sand and rock mountain. The expression should be dignified and gentle, with deep, far seeing eyes."

Opposite, top left: A traditional tobacconist store in Manama's old suq features whole dry leaves of tobacco and locally made hubble-bubble pipes. (Pradhan).

Opposite, top right: Locally made hubble-bubble pipes are a popular means of tobacco smoking. (Pradhan).

Opposite, bottom: Caged birds are a familiar sight at Manama's old suq. (Pradhan).

Right: A traditionally dressed Bahraini girl assists with the date harvest. (Falcon).

Below: Featuring many of the requirements of a traditional household, this hardware store in Manama's old suq preserves the flavour of an Eastern bazaar. (Vine).

Above: Beautifully carved wooden doors of Manama's old Law Courts now open into the compound of the Directorate of Heritage. (Vine).

Right: Demonstrating the traditional rope plaiting techniques used to fabricate pearl-diving equipment (in this case the ring surrounding the opening of a pearl-shell bag) a retired pearl fisherman recalls Bahrain's maritime traditions. (Directorate of Cultural Heritage and Museums).

Opposite, top left: Plaiting a belt from strips of dried palm leaf, this lady upholds Bahrain's rich cultural traditions. (Directorate of Heritage and Museums).

Opposite, bottom: The traditional sword-dance is frequently performed on ceremonial occasions as a mark of respect to visiting dignitaries. (Directorate of Heritage and Museums).

Opposite, top right: (Directorate of Heritage and Museums).

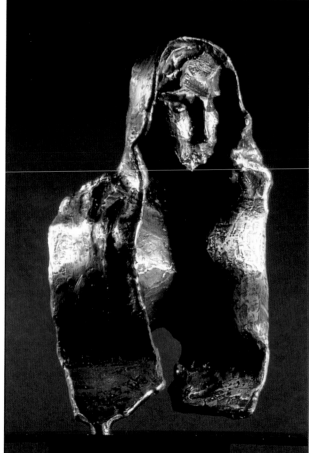

Islamic Calligraphy. Fibreglass. Ali Al-Mahmeed.

Right: Bronze sculpture, "Eve". Hassan al-Sahaf

*Bahrain Arts Society provides a venue for many artists and art
lovers in Bahrain. The Society holds regular exhibitions of local
artists' work.* Bahrain Arts Society.

ART & ARTISTS

The islands of Bahrain have been a rich source of literary and artistic inspiration throughout history. Today's thriving artistic community draws upon all aspects of the country and its people in creating art forms which not only capture the unique flavour and atmosphere of Bahrain, but also make a strong statement in the creative world at large. Local artists have been actively encouraged by the Bahrain Government. In 1982 the Bahrain Minister of Information, H.E. Tariq Almoayed proposed the creation of a Bahrain Arts Society and supported the artistic community in the establishment of an arts and cultural centre. The Society is now a flourishing organisation housed in a tastefully appointed, Spanish-style building off the Budaiya road. Although it was not built for the purpose, the design is almost perfect for the Society's dual role of promotion and education. Exhibitions are regularly held in the spacious halls, while adults and children alike have the opportunity to develop their creativity in a wide variety of visual art classes. Tuition is offered by enthusiastic and talented volunteers in such fields as oil painting, pottery, sculpture, Arabic calligraphy, photography and interior design. The Arts Society is a spiritual, social and physical meeting place for artists and art-lovers; a rare and welcome phenomena in a world where all too often artists and their patrons or admirers live a segregated existence.

On viewing the work of Bahrain artists one is immediately aware of a strong individuality of style, suggesting quiet confidence in each artists vision of his or her world. In spite of this diversity there is a harmony between abstraction and realism; between fibreglass and oils, that derives fom an underlying organic sensitivity in each creation. One is left with the impression of a mellifluous blending between old and new, and between natural and man-made — a blending which is an accurate reflection of Bahrain today. Perhaps it is this which has made exhibitions of Bahrain art so popular in othe parts of the world. Collective and individual exhibitions of Bahrain artists have been viewed and acclaimed in many countries including France, Britain, India, Singapore, Morocco, Egypt, Kuwait, Jordan, and the United States. The educational background of the artists is equally impressive and includes graduates from the Beaux Arts in Paris; the Parson School of Art and Design in New York and the College of Fine Arts in Cairo. It is perfectly evident from their work that the artists have a firm grounding in draftsmanship and composition and I discussed this point with Shaikh Rashid Al-Khalifa, President of the Arts Society. An accomplished artist himself, he has played a key role in organising the Arts Society and in encouraging young people to benefit from the opportunities for training and shared experiences which the society offers. On the subject of style in art he expressed to me his view that there is a place for all schools in the context of 'Bahrain Art' but that he believes that the artist should start with a solid grounding in drawing techniques. "Whatever modern style a painting or sculpture may take it is important that the artist should have an ability, regardless of whether this is expressed in the particular work of art, to depict an object in its geometric form. By this I mean that he or she should be able to sit down and draw a cup or a vase in the form of a reasonably accurate representation of the object. This is where art begins and once the artist has mastered such basic skills there is plenty of scope to branch out into a particular style.' Sheikh Rashid followed these comments by escorting me around an exhibition of young artists currently on display in the main gallery of the Arts Centre. One could not have failed to be impressed by the artists' grasp of composition, perspective, tone and colour in their use of a variety of materials to create pencil sketches, water colours, oil-paintings and several sculptures. Such a wealth of talent among the beginners school of artists is further evidence for the natural artistic ability of many Bahrainis. Opportunities for artists to earn their living from art are however limited and most of Bahrain's artists practice in a part-time capacity treating their creative work more as a hobby or means of relaxing rather than a full-time occupation. One of the exceptions to this generalisation is a talented member of Bahrain's art community: Ab-

dullah Ahmed Al-Muharraqi whose painting of pearl divers is reproduced on page 115. Muharraqi is a founder member of what he describes as Bahrain's Formative Art School. His paintings portray natural and traditional aspects of Bahrain life, dealing with subjects such as pearl-harvesting; falconing; village scenes; folk dancing; Arabian hospitality and so on. His clear, bold style is ideal for the subjects he portrays and his personal involvement with, and love for, Bahrain shows in his work; particularly in his portraits of Bahrainis. In addition to painting and exhibiting such canvases, Muharraqi has designed stamps for Bahrain and is a regular cartoonist for Akhbar Al-Khaleej, a local Arabic newspaper.

It would be wrong however to single out any particular artist from Bahrain as being of more importance than others since artistic creation is very much alive and there are many artists whose work is less well known than others but whose talent is just as great. The selection of paintings and sculptures shown here has been kindly provided by Bahrain Arts Society to whom I am indebted for their assistance and for the opportunity they provided for me to become acquainted with the art and artists of Bahrain.

Pearl Diver's Tragedy. Oil painting. Abdullah Al-Muharraqi.

Bahrain Arts Society

Covered Bazaar. Oil painting. Abbas Al-Moosawi.

Bahrain Arts Society

Heritage. Oil painting. Abbas Al-Mahroos.

Bahrain Arts Society

Old market scene. Rashid Al-Khalifa.

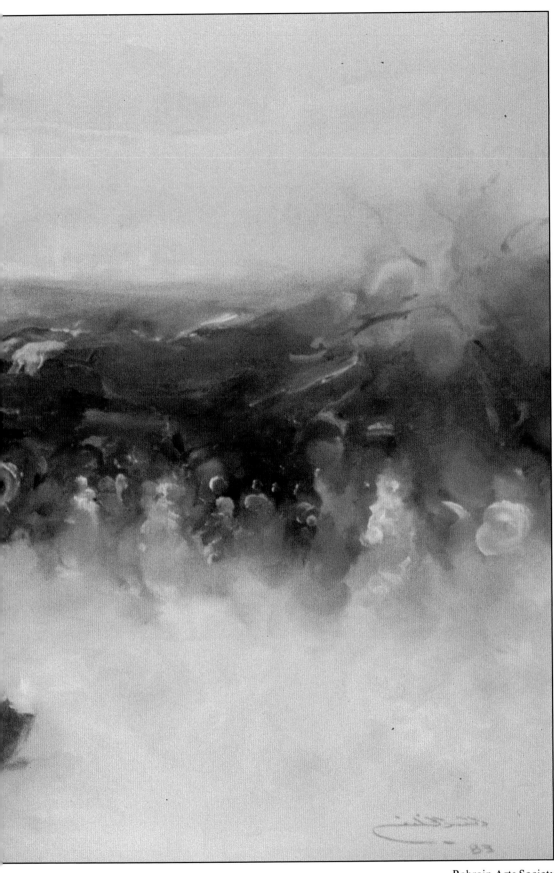

Bahrain Arts Society

Old town. Mousa Al-Aali.

Bahrain Arts Society

Oud Player. Rashid Al-Khalifa.

Bahrain Arts Society

Flower pot. Oil painting. Ishiq Kooheji.   Bahrain Arts Society

Girl. Oil painting. Ahmed Guhloom.

Bahrain Arts Society

Oasis. Oil painting. Abdul Rahmin Sharif.

Bahrain Arts Society

Suq scene. Oil painting. Abdul Rahmin Sharif.

Bahrain Arts Society

Low-tide. Rashid Sawar.

Bahrain Arts Society

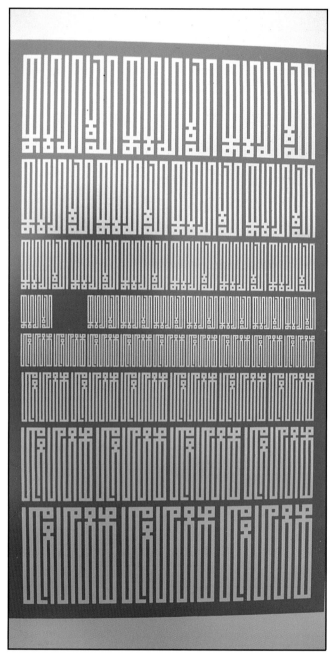

Calligraphy. Abdul Ellah Alarab   Bahrain Art Society.

Kitchen table. Joanna Ting.

Bahrain Arts Society

Bronze sculpture, "Two in One". Hassan al-Sahaf   Bahrain Arts Society

Symphony. Oil painting. Hussain Alsunni.

Bahrain Arts Society

A winter scene 1. Oil painting. Abdul L. Muffez.   Bahrain Arts Society

A winter scene 2. Oil painting. Abdul L. Muffez.

Bahrain Arts Society

Right: Crustbreaker in operation at one of ALBA's pot-rooms, (ALBA).

Below: Construction of the customs island on the Saudi-Bahrain causeway. (Ballast-Nedam).

Opposite: Spring sky. (Vine).

Opposite, bottom: Pearl Pedestal (Vine).

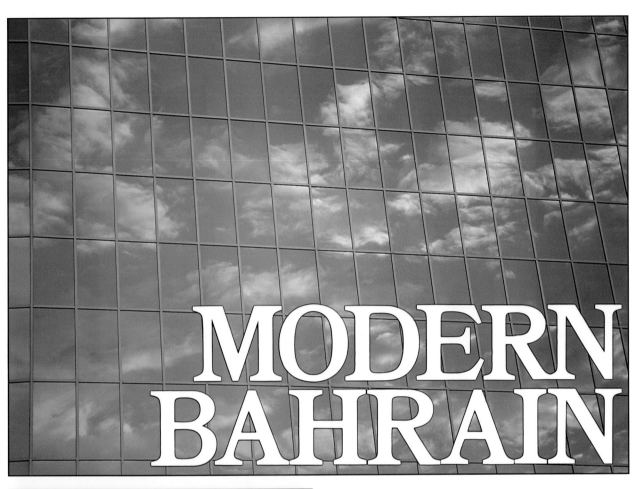

MODERN BAHRAIN

The construction of the Saudi-Bahrain causeway re-establishes a land-link between mainland Arabia and Bahrain fractured by a rise in sea-level 7,000 years ago. At that time Bahrain was a wild, low-lying stretch of land blessed by large natural springs of fresh-water nourishing several fertile oases in an otherwise arid landscape. The modern, 25 kilometer land-bridge is an engineering marvel, a fitting tribute to the tremendous strides made by both countries during the current century. Astute management of natural resources have provided the finance to create outstanding infra-structures culminating in this visionary proposal. The selected design not only reenacted prehistoric links but also sought to satisfy the exigencies of the marine environment by utilising widely spaced concrete pilons permitting tidal currents to maintain water exchange and thus minimising any deleterious effects on marine ecosystems. The contract was awarded to the Dutch company, Ballast Nedam, on July 8th, 1981. The completed causeway carries a four lane highway with central reserve, safety lanes and hard shoulder. It snakes across the shallow Gulf waters from the north-eastern Bahrain village of Jasra to the Saudi Arabian coastal settlement of Al-Aziziyah, 10 kilometres south of Al Khobar. Enroute from Bahrain's main island to Saudi Arabia, the causeway traverses the Bahrain island of Um Nassan, until now a renowned sanctuary for herds of gazelle and other wildlife. There are five separate bridges in the causeway with individual lengths of 934, 3334, 5194, 2034 and 934 metres respectively. Bridge No. 3 (5,194 metres long) has a main span of 150 metres (cf. 50m on others) and a clear headway of 28.5m allowing large ships to navigate successfully via the deep-water channel. Both the bridges and supporting piles are made of pre-stressed concrete and the heaviest member, one of the prefabricated concrete superstructural elements, weighs about 1,300 tons! Such an awesome statistic is but one gigantic facet of an entirely colossal scale. In actual fact every individual aspect of the project arouses an overwhelming sense of wonder. During my visit to the site-office on the central island in the spring of 1986, a high mountain of sand, dredged from the Gulf towered over scurrying "dinky-toy" trucks ferrying it to the mainland. As I waited to pass through the security check at the causeway's entrance one truck passed-by every six seconds with no let-up or break in the frenetic sequence! The heavy laden vehicles roared past in a cloud of dust, dumped their sand at the approach road construction site about half a mile from the entrance gate, and then returned to the causeway to collect a new load. Statistics on such projects are always difficult to translate into reality but I cannot resist quoting one more to underline the awe inspiring magnitude of this most impressive project; five million tons of material were used in building the causeway which has earned the tag of the World's most expensive stretch of road.

Primarily the causeway was forged as a gesture of friendship between Saudi Arabia and Bahrain and a means of cementing the close ties which exist between the two countries. The fact that one can now drive direct from Bahrain to Saudi Arabia, Asia or Europe will have a considerable influence on commercial links and tourism. Bahrain looks to the causeway as an important step towards consolidating its future.

Bahrain's first oil-well at Jebel ad Dukhan (Vine).

The transformation effected in Bahrain in the twentieth century must be greater than that experienced by most developing countries. Whereas, in the early 1900's Bahrain still depended largely on its pearling industry and its infrastructure was rudimentary, eighty years later the State is regarded as one of the most up-to-date of Arabian nations boasting a well organised administration and many examples of outstandingly unique and stylish architecture. Housing projects provide a good standard of accommodation for all Bahrainis; education and medical facilities are highly developed and the State is leading the field in communications systems.

This rapid progress was funded at first by the pearling industry but, as this diminished in importance, oil was discovered and the hydrocarbon industry took over its role as the mainstay of Bahrain's economy. It was, in fact, the first country surrounding the Gulf to have an oil-based economy. In the mid 1920's few people believed that commercial quantities of oil were to be found in the region. Major Frank Holmes a New Zealand entrepreneur representing "Eastern and General Syndicate" was however deeply convinced of Bahrain's hidden wealth. His syndicate, having been granted the first oil concession in 1925, was however short of funds for exploration and development. They had tried to sell shares to several large UK companies including the British Government but their approaches were repulsed. Finally, in 1927 the American pioneering oil company: Eastern Gulf acquired an option on the licence and despatched a British geologist, Ralph Roades to investigate. As it became apparent that the concessions encompassed a real oil-field, interest grew and by the end of 1928 the Standard Oil Company of California had obtained rights over the concession. Shortly afterwards the Bahrain Petroleum Company (BAPCO) was formed as a subsidiary of SOCAL. A general supervisor by the name of William F. Taylor and a young geologist called Fred Davies were SOCAL's first people in the field. Davies' survey showed immediate promise and a pioneering SOCAL drilling crew arrived on May 26th 1931. Just over four months later they commenced drilling near Jebel ad-Dukhan ("Mountain of Smoke") and on June 1st 1932 — almost exactly a year after setting foot on the island, oil began flowing at a rate of 9,600 barrels per day! The region's number one oil-well is preserved to this day and makes an interesting focal point for a visit. The Jebel ad-Dukhan strike finally convinced the sceptics and thus

began the major oil exploration programme leading to the discovery of the World's richest petroleum deposits in Saudi Arabia and the Gulf States. Shaikh Hamed granted a mining lease to BAPCO on December 29th 1934 and this paved the way for the establishment of an integrated oil industry in Bahrain.

The discovery of Bahrain's oil reserves came at an opportune point in time. Oil revenues softened the impact of the collapse in the natural pearl industry and the widespread depression which deeply affected the World economy. They also permitted an acceleration in growth but since oil reserves are not inexhaustible the Government of Bahrain has continuously planned for a new future where income will be derived from sources other than natural hydrocarbon reserves. Between the occasion of the first oil strike in 1932 and 1985, three hundred and twenty-five oil wells were sunk on the relatively small field at Jebel ad-Dukhan. These yielded more than 684 million barrels of oil but since 1970 production rates from the field have been on the decline from a peak of 76,000 barrels per day to a 1984 level of 44,022 bpd.

Overall oil production in 1984 stabilised at 15.3 million barrels. The downward trend evident for thirteen years had been finally halted as a result of enhanced recovery techniques including gas injection to maintain reservoir pressure in the oil-producing zones. At the same time offshore exploration

continues and Bahrain also benefits from its 50 percent share of revenues derived from the Abu Saafa field adjacent to the Saudi-Bahrain boundary line, on the Saudi Arabian side.

Oil refining began in 1935 and the processing of crude oil since the early stages of Bahrain's oil drilling programme has ensured that maximum economic benefits accrue to the country from its oil resources. From an initial level of 10,800 bpd the refining capacity has grown to more than quarter of a million barrels per day. Oil from both Bahrain and Saudi Arabia is processed into a wide range of products including diesel fuels (18 grades); gasoline (30 grades); naphthas (9 grades); fuel oils (16 grades) and liquefied petroleum gas (LPG). In all there are 84 grades of products processed at the refinery. The oil from Saudi Arabia is carried via the 34 mile long Saudi Arabia-Bahrain pipeline, the fore-runner of which was a twelve inch bore, seventeen mile long pipe laid in 1945 — at that time the world's longest commercial submarine pipeline!

Bahrain's oil industry is now managed by the Bahrain National Oil Company — BANOCO — a fully integrated company responsible for all aspects of oil and gas exploitation from exploration and drilling to distribution and marketing both locally and internationally. Oil from BANOCO's production is refined at BAPCO's Sitra refinery which is majority owned by the Bahrain Government. Products are exported to countries such as UAE, Singapore, Japan and many other venues on tankers loaded at the Sitra deepwater oil terminal. Here work continues around the clock and an average of three to four ships per day are loaded at the six marine berths.

Whereas oil production has been gradually falling for a number of years (with a recent stabilisation of this trend); natural gas production has been steadily increasing as a result of the development of the Khuff Gas reservoir as well as gas production in association with oil extraction. In 1984 production of natural gas and associated gas averaged 532 million cubic feet per day. By early 1986 21 Khuff gas wells and 20 dehydrating units were on stream with a daily capacity of more than one billion standard cubic feet of dry gas! It has been estimated that if current extraction rates are maintained, Bahrain's natural gas reserves will hold up for about fifty years. Thus, despite the increase of recent years the long-term trend will once again show a decline in production. Bahrain is now investigating the possibility of locating new reserves of both oil and gas which will provide a longer-term stability for its hydrocarbon industry.

Bahrain's gas production and processing is operated by BANAGAS, a company established by the Bahrain Government in 1979. A huge gas liquids plant built by the Japan Gasoline Company is processing 124 million cubic feet of feed gas per day. In 1983, 1,004,882 net barrels of propane; 911,526 barrels of butane and 1,232,349 barrels of naphtha were produced. A total gas production (ie. associated gas plus natural gas) in 1984 was 195.4 billion cubic feet, a five per cent increase on the 1983 figure.

Apart from oil and gas production the aluminium smelter which began production in May 1971 is Bahrain's longest established non-oil industrial project. The decision to situate the smelter in Bahrain was based firstly upon the need to diversify the country's economic base; secondly on the local availability of natural gas and thirdly upon the fact that Bahrain is roughly half-way between Western Australia's bauxite reserves and the markets for aluminium in Europe. Production is carried out by Aluminium Bahrain, otherwise known as ALBA which is majority owned by the Bahrain Government. The plant has a capacity of approximately 170,000 tonnes per year which is produced in the form of standard ingots (1985: 116,210 tonnes; rolling ingots 2,024 tonnes); extrusion billet (1983: 16,289 tonnes) and tee ingots (1983: 13,747 tonnes). Aluminium from

Below: Unloading Aluminium at dusk at ALBA's marine terminal. (ALBA).

Opposite: Standard ingots of Aluminium manufactured by Bahrain's Aluminium Company, ALBA. (ALBA).

the plant is marketed by the Bahrain Saudi Aluminium Marketing Company which today sells to customers in more than 20 countries, especially in the Middle East, South East Asia and the Far East. ALBA's production of raw aluminium has led to a number of satellite industries being established on Bahrain. Bahrain Atomisers was the first of these, converting molten aluminium to fine grade aluminium powder to be utilised in a range of activities from paint production to explosives manufacture. Midal cables, the second venture, makes aluminium rod and insulated overhead conductors to a very high standard. It is also the largest single user of ALBAS aluminium production. A new associated project is that of the Gulf Aluminium Rolling Mill (GARMCO) with an annual capacity of 40,000 tons. This is a joint venture operation owned by the Gulf Aluminium Rolling Company whose share-holders include Bahrain (20%); Saudi Arabia (20%); Kuwait (20%); Iraq (20%); Oman (10%) and Qatar (10%). The company hot-rolls slabs of aluminium provided by ALBA and produces 6mm thick sheets of aluminium which are then cold-rolled into various products such as sheets, circles and corrugated sheets.

Another satellite industry which is based upon

ALBA's production of aluminium is an extrusion plant owned by the Bahrain Aluminium Extrusion Company (BALEXCO) producing doors, window frames, cladding etc. for the construction industry. It produces a number of fine quality products including some coated with polyester powder and available in a wide range of colours. The company's annual output of 5,000 tons is committed a year in advance!

Encouraged by the success of Bahrain's first metal industrial development in the form of ALBA and its satellite operations the Arab Iron and Steel Company E.C. (AISCO) was incorporated in 1980 as an offshore public shareholding company. The initial offering of shares to the public was forty three times over subscribed! The company has constructed an iron pelletising plant with a capacity of 4 million tons per year. It imports ore fines from several sources (notably South America; Mauritania and India) and processes these into iron oxide pellets which are exported to Saudi Arabia; Iraq; Qatar and other parts of the world. Once again however, the company is likely to spawn a number of satellite industries and there is little doubt that there will be other large downstream industries established in the coming years.

Opposite: Operating the overhead crane in the pot-room at Bahrain's Aluminium Company, ALBA. (ALBA).

Left: BATELCO's Satellite Earth Stations provide links to the International Telecommunications Satellite Organisation's (INTELSAT's) worldwide communications network and to ARABSAT, the Arab World's own satellite system. (BATELCO).

A new petrochemical complex on Sitra island is scheduled to produce the staggering figure of 1,000 tons of ammonia and methanol per day! Eighty three percent of the ammonia is to be used in fertiliser production. The project is owned by the Bahrain Government; SABIC (Saudi Basic Industries Corporation) and Kuwait's Petrochemical Industries Company. Bahrain's development has not centred solely on the heavy section. Apart from the satellite ventures associated with ALBA's production of aluminium, a number of other light industry projects have been established. Bahrain Light Industries Company for example is working close to its full capacity of 65,000 pieces of furniture per year.

The technological and industrial development of Bahrain has taken place at a staggering rate. To fully understand progress made in communications I visited the headquarters of Bahrain Telecommunications Company and spoke to Ali Sahwan, public relations officer for the company. He explained that Bahrain's telecommunications were first established as part of the Indo-European undersea telegraph cable link-up in 1964 and since then Bahrain has been at the forefront of innovation and development in this field. Today BATELCO

operates three Satellite Earth Communications Stations and one of the most up to date telephone systems in the world. The first ever multi-channel intercontinental radio link from the Middle East to the world, consisting of the Satellite Earth Station at Ras Abu Jarjur was established in 1969. The first conversation via the important new link-up took place between His Highness the Amir, Shaikh Isa bin Salman Al-Khalifa and Prince Philip. This major step forward was followed by a wide range of improvements including the advent of international direct dialling which we tend to take for granted today. Service has been further enhanced through a number of developments including the inauguration of digital exchanges; an additional Satellite Earth Communications installation (bringing the system in line with standard A specifications of the International Telecommunications Satellite Organisation: INTELSAT); the opening of Telephone House and Telegraph House and the inauguration of specialised service such as advanced radio phones; paging systems; public card phones; private international communications services and access to several hundred USA data bases. Progress to date has clearly underlined the Bahrain Government's firm commitment to maintenance of top class telecommunications. As further evidence of this one must point to Bahrain's participation in the ARABSAT project consisting of two communications satellites providing 8,000 new telephone channels to the region. Apart from voice communications ARABSAT offers a range of other services such as regional, domestic and community TV distribution; video conferencing; electronic mail service; data collection from remote recording instruments; airline bookings; simultaneous newspaper printing and exchange of aeronautical navigational data.

I was somewhat surprised to learn that, despite Bahrain's plethora of impressive modern telecommunication systems, direct link-ups via submarine cables still have a role to play. Ali Sahwan explained that submarine links have been established between Bahrain, Qatar and the U.A.E. Apart from the improved clarity which such links can provide they also have important security advantages.

But, I asked him, where does BATELCO go from here? Have we reached the zenith so far as telecommunications are concerned? "Far from it", he answered, "the next step will be for further improvements in quality of transmission on all

systems and I can forsee a day when we will all have television screens and data terminals in our living rooms. We will be able to receive up to the minute news; have push-button control of financial transactions; and have access via viewphone facilities to a wide range of home education opportunities". Having had a clearer line to my remote home on the west coast of Ireland than I have ever achieved on local calls to locations a few miles apart, I was already impressed before I visited BATELCO, but by the time I left I was also entirely envious if not downright covetous. There is no doubt that the standard of telecommunications which BATELCO has achieved is a key factor in attracting many of the offshore international businesses to relocate in Bahrain.

Efficient telecommunications were a "sine qua non" for the establishment of Bahrain's numerous OBU's (offshore banking units). Foreign banks were encouraged to set-up office in Bahrain by a number of factors. Firstly, regulative incentives such as exemption from maintaining reserves with the Bahrain Monetary Agency; the absence of depositor's with-holding tax on interest earned; and income-tax exemption. Secondly, general working and living conditions were acceptable for foreign staff. For

Right: The new headquarters of the Bank of Bahrain and Kuwait, while under construction (Vine)

Opposite: Evening light and the Manama skyline. (Vine).

Bahrain the growth in offshore banking facilities and subsequent development as a service centre for Gulf and Arab countries represents further diversification within the economy.

The banks themselves provide a range of services including deposit facilities; foreign exchange transactions; overseas trade financing and the provision of performance and guarantee bonds. In addition they organise medium and long-term loans, often in syndication with other banks, and they participate in bond issues. Their presence in Bahrain has provided a key incentive for the establishment of many "exempt companies" which in turn have boosted the service industry sector in the local economy.

Locally referred to as "BBK", the Bank of Bahrain and Kuwait is an excellent example of a Middle East bank which has adapted to the rapid developments of the region's economy. At the time of writing a new building is under construction which will house the bank's Bahrain headquarters. It is a magnificently sited and brilliantly conceived structure in which the upper stories are suspended above an open area

created by adjacent wings of the buildings. The unique design shades seaward facing windows while leaving enviable, unobscured views of the nearby gulf.

BBK provides a number of innovative services for investors, both locally and internationally. They have for example a high yielding, quick access foreign currency saving account which has proved popular with many expatriates. On the International front BBK has branches in Kuwait, India, Turkey and an affiliated branch in Oman. While it is true that there has been a down-turn in business and profits for many local ventures, Rashid Abdul Rahman Al Zayani, Chairman of BBK speaks for many of Bahrain's bankers when he comments:

"I remain convinced that we are in the right business, in the right locations, bringing the right kind of services to the public."

The importance of education and training to equip Bahrainis for work in banking has led to the establishment of a Banker's Training Centre in Bahrain. This was opened in 1980 and the 1985 intake included 1,700 students who enrolled in 18 different courses!

Opposite and left: Recently restored to its original splendour, Bab al Bahrain situated in the heart of Manama, provides a passage to the older quarter of the city. (Vine).

Below: Charcoal, sunflower seeds, peanuts, hazelnuts, and almonds are displayed by the sack-full on pavements in Manama's traditional shopping area. (Vine).

Bab Al Bahrain is a recently restored elegant white building adorned with narrow twin widows and a broad archway through which one passes, as if by time machine, from the ultra modern environment along Manama's main coast road to the bustling romantic Eastern atmosphere created by crowded narrow streets and open-fronted stores stocking a cosmopolitan array from oriental spices to electronic gadgetry. Here, bartering seems to be almost an end in itself so that the bargain must be pursued at all costs. Foreigners can move freely through the busy streets of this charming bazaar enjoying the dazzling diversity of its wares without fear of harassment. The response of shop-keepers and fellow shoppers alike is unfailingly one of courteous hospitality creating a relaxed atmosphere within the richly Arabian ethnocentric environment.

Bab al Bahrain is itself a relatively new building, designed as Government Offices by Sir Charles Belgrave in 1945. At that time it was not so far from the water's edge and overlooked Custom's Square and the pier. By the mid-1950's land reclamation had

pushed out the coastline and provided the new ground on which all the modern buildings on the seaward side of Government Avenue have been built. In the early part of this century Manama's wharf area (just opposite Bab al Bahrain) was an extremely colourful scene with fleets of dhows moored a short distance from the pier attracting seamen from all over the Gulf and from farther afield. Sir Charles Belgrave recalled the fascination of the place in his book: "Personal Column" where he wrote:

"... There were stocky, dark men from Sur, below Muscat, wearing ochre coloured clothes, yellow headcloths or red skull caps; lean, long-haired Muscatis with hawklike features, often accompanied by one or two lascivious youths; Persians, wearing tall felt hats loose, full-sleeved robes, with wide woolen shawls round their waists and Indians from the Malabar coast who came ashore from their big sailing ships, which were usually the largest in the port. Often the Indians brought with them little green parrots in cages to sell to the Arabs. Longboats, full of men who sang as they rowed, moved between the dhows and the pierhead, and coolies shouted and sang as they shouldered heavy sacks, loading and unloading cargo of every conceivable kind."

In her guide-book entitled "The Islands of Bahrain" Angela Clark provides instructions for a number of tours around Bahrain including one which follows the old shoreline of Manama and takes in its most historic sites allowing one to relive the stirring scenes described by historians such as Belgrave.

Shoppers in Bahrain are unlikely to be disappointed for Manama boasts some of the best stocked shops in the Middle East. There are several ultra-modern shopping centres where it is as much a pleasure to admire the artistic window displays as it is to actually buy something. Then there are also the smaller stores of the Suq area which specialise in a variety of goods and finally one can visit the open-air markets.

After passing through the gateway, the walk up Bab al Bahrain road continues into the suq and, after a few hundred metres, to the most fascinating of all — the Gold Suq. The entrance to the main gold selling street is marked by the corner gold shop of K. Al Fardan and, usually, by a policeman standing on the corner. A left turn at this point brings one into a street packed with gold jewellery and pearl shops. Not far along, on the left, the new indoor Bahrain Gold Suq building is situated. This has an ultra modern marble floored interior in which one can browse in comfort, away from the glare of summer sun and where all Bahrain's major jewellers are represented. There are four levels of arcades with, on the ground floor, a cafe where shoppers can enjoy light refreshments.

In contrast to the frenetic Eastern aura surrounding the street shops, all here is cool air-conditioned sophistication replete with escalators and ultra-modern decor but the traditional gold jewellery and strings of pearls are no less attractive or unique. Shop windows sparkle under drapes of gold necklaces, bracelets and other jewellery — an exhibition of stylish affluence one would rarely witness elsewhere in the world. Such a scintillating display can be unnerving to the vacillating customer and how one finally settles upon which item of jewellery to purchase, and from whom, must be more a matter of chance than design.

Opposite: Manama sky. (Pradhan).

Right: Manama at night (Pradhan).

Below: An evening to fish. (Pradhan).

The best way to explore this area is to set-off in the afternoon, when the shops are open, and to wander more or less at random, taking time to observe both the shops and shoppers. Whether one is browsing in small traditional shops or in modern indoor arcades one will find the same warm welcome and experience the same genuine hospitality for which Bahrain and its people have become so justifiably famous.

Over the years, Bahrain has demonstrated a unique talent for overcoming various obstacles to its development. When the pearl industry slumped, oil took over; when oil reserves dwindled natural gas discoveries provided a reprieve; when the price of oil fell the country was able to reflect upon the wisdom of its diversification policies; as groundwater reserves deteriorated a desalination programme provided a solution based upon use of its energy resources. A great deal of Bahrain's success has been based, over the centuries, upon astute management of its affairs by the Government of the day. Despite its insular status since earliest times it has been extremely wide-ranging in its contacts. Today, Bahrain continues to exert a positive influence for reconciliation, stability, peace, prosperity and well being of all Arabian countries. It may have changed greatly since its Dilmun era but the islands of Bahrain have retained their distinctive character and have fully justified their description as **"Pearls in Arabian Waters"**.

ACKNOWLEDGEMENTS

The task of writing this book and compiling the illustrations has brought me in contact with many people whom I had not previously met and with whom I have established firm friendships. This has been one of the most rewarding aspects of what has been an entirely enjoyable assignment. Everybody with whom I have discussed the book has been most helpful and in many cases their assistance extended beyond the bounds of what might have been considered their official duty. It is therefore a great pleasure to thank here some of the people and organisations who have played a part in the completion of this publication.

Firstly, I must thank the Bahrain Government and H.E. Tariq Almoayed, The Minister of Information who originally proposed to me that IMMEL should produce a book on Bahrain and then welcomed me as author and coordinator of the project. I am most grateful to him for his personal interest and encouragement. Much of my work in Bahrain would have been impossible without the advice and introductions which I received from Mr. Ahmed Al Sherooqi, Director of Public Relations and Media in the Ministry of Information. Also under the aegis of the Ministry of Information, I received considerable assistance from Shaikha Nayla Ali Khalifa, Director of Heritage; Shaikh Rashid Al-Khalifa, Director of Tourism and Archaeology and their respective staff.

Several organisations deserve special mention. The Bahrain Arts Society and its President, Shaikh Rashid Al-Khalifa, were extremely helpful in providing me with the work of a number of Bahrain artists and in freely discussing the work of the Society. I was deeply impressed by the true sense of purpose and dedication displayed by members of the Arts Society and hope that the Arts section of this book conveys something of the talent and energy which exists within Bahrain's artistic community. The other Society which proved to be of enormous help was the Bahrain Natural History Society. The first member of the Society whom I met was Tom Nightingale who, not too surprisingly turned out to be a dedicated ornithologist. Tom has played a key role in running the Natural History Society and he had no hesitation in introducing me to other members of the society who were able to help in a variety of ways. In addition Tom kindly provided me with the impressive series of annual reports by the Bahrain Natural History Society. These provide the caucus for much of our knowledge of Bahrain's wildlife. I am indebted to Tom and to the Society as a whole for permission to draw on some of this information in compiling the chapter on natural history. One of the most important contributions to this book is the superb collection of wild-life photographs provided by BNHS member Dr. Mike Hill who not only took the pictures but also wrote scientific captions to accompany them.

In my search for references on Bahrain's past I visited the library of the British Council in Bahrain and was assisted there by Mrs. Jean Basheer. I also visited the Biology Department of University College of Bahrain where the Department Head: Dr. Saeed Abdulla kindly introduced me to his staff with whom

I held interesting discussions on Bahrain's natural history. I was also fortunate enough to meet Professor Phil Basson who advised me concerning research activities taking place in the area and introduced me to Walter Vreeland, Senior Advisor to the Bahrain Environmental Protection Technical Secretariat and also to Dr. David Vousden of the same organisation. Both these members of EPTS were extremely helpful in providing me with information on the marine environment around Bahrain and with data concerning their own research. The EPTS is carrying out a vital function in an area where the pressures for rapid change and large scale development are often overbearing. They have worked closely with industrial projects and planners to ensure that the environment is, so far as possible, protected. Were it not for such efforts it would not have been possible to portray such a positive picture of Bahrain's wildlife as occurs in these pages. If this book helps to achieve an increase in the awareness of both general public and official planners regarding the importance of a continued commitment to wildlife conservation then I believe that the support which EPTS and others have given to my work will have been well rewarded.

The contribution which Al Areen wildlife park and reserve has made to natural conservation in Bahrain is already well known and deserves the highest praise. In the context of this book, I am most grateful to Dr. Edgar Allonby, from Al Areen who organised my visit to the project, as well as the open reserve for oryx and gazelle which they operate at Hawar. On both visits I was accompanied by Dr. Kate Monk whose work on Gazelle provided me with a wonderful introduction to terrestrial field-studies of Bahrain's ecology.

I am also pleased to acknowledge help from a number of other quarters. For information and photographs of dugongs, I am grateful to Dr. Tony Preen and the Saudi Arabian Meteorological and Environmental Protection Administration. For some useful guidance around Bahrain, I am most grateful for the assistance of Bahrain Explored and their enthusiastic and well informed guide; Elsa Cook. For a brief, but valuable discussion regarding the book's title and contents I am grateful to Mr. Leif Munksgaard of Family Bookship, Bahrain.

I have pleasure to thank Paula McHenry for some valuable liaison in Bahrain. Major photographic contributors are separately listed but I should add that the public relations sections of several companies were most helpful. In particular I should mention Ballast Nedam; BATELCO; ALBA; Bank of Bahrain and Kuwait; and BANOCO.

I am indebted to designer and illustrator Jane Stark for her excellent lay-out and design as well as for her willing assistance with all aspects of this book's production.

Finally, I wish to thank my family; Paula for her editorial assistance and my daughters Catriona, Sinead and Megan who showed great patience with my long absences from home and with the prolonged periods of seclusion during which I researched and wrote this book.

REFERENCES

Al Khalifa, Shaikha Haya Ali and Michael Rice. BAHRAIN THROUGH THE AGES, KPI 1986. NOTE: Separate papers from this valuable publication are not listed here. The reader is recommended to refer to this text for detailed information regarding recent archaeological surveys of Bahrain and for its comprehensive bibliography.

Allen, M. FALCONRY IN ARABIA, Orbis, 1980.

Bahrain Natural History Society. Annual reports, 1976 to 1984.

Basson, P.W. et al. BIOTOPES OF THE WESTERN ARABIAN GULF. ARAMCO, 1977.

Belgrave, Sir Charles PERSONAL COLUMN, Hutchinson, London 1960.

Bent, J. Theodore "The Bahrain Islands in the Persian Gulf". Proc. Royal Geographic Society, XII, 1890.

Bibby, Geoffrey LOOKING FOR DILMUN. Collins (London) 1970; Pelican Books (London) 1972.

Clarke, Angela 1981. THE ISLANDS OF BAHRAIN. Bahrain Historical and Archaeological Society.

Doornkamp, J.C., D. Brunsden, D.K.C. Jones (Ed) "Geology, Geomorphology and Pedology of Bahrain" Geo Abstracts Ltd., Univesity of East Anglia, UK. 1980.

Durand, Capt. E.L. "The Islands and Antiquities of Bahrain" (with notes by Maj. Gen. Sir H.C. Rawlinson). Journal of the Royal Society (New Series), XII, (Part II) 1880, pp. 189-227.

During Caspers, E.C.L. Harappan Trade in the Arabian Gulf in the 3rd Millennium B.C. DILMUN 5. December 1973.

Farmer, A.S.D. and Docksey, J.E. A bibliography of the marine and maritime environment of the Arabian Gulf and Gulf of Oman, Kuwait. Bull. Mar. Sci. 4: 1-121.

Fisheries Statistical Service, Technical Circulars and fisheries statistical reports for 1984 and 1985.

Gallagher, M. and D.L. Harrison. The Terrestrial Mammals of Bahrain, Journal Bombay Nat. Hist. Soc. Vol. 72.2. pp407-421.

Good, R.D.'O. The Bahrain islands and their desert flora. Proc. Symp. Inst. of Biol. 1954, vol. 152, 45-55.

Harrison, D.L. MAMMALS OF THE GULF. George Allen and Unwin, 1981.

Hawk Publishing. THE BUSINESSMAN'S HOTEL ROOM GUIDE TO BAHRAIN 1984-85.

Hill, M. and P. Webb AN INTRODUCTION TO THE WILDLIFE OF BAHRAIN, Bahrain Ministry of Information.

Jones, David A. A FIELD GUIDE TO THE SEA SHORES OF KUWAIT AND THE ARABIAN GULF, University of Kuwait, 1986.

Lipscombe Vincett, B.A. WILDFLOWERS OF SAUDI ARABIA. Immel 1984.

Prideaux, F.B. The Sepulchral Tumuli of Bahrain, Archaeological Survey of India — Annual Report, 1908-1909, pp60-78.

Price, A.R.G. Echinoderms of Saudi Arabia etc. Fauna of Saudi Arabia 4. 3-21, 1982.

Randall, J.E. SHARKS OF ARABIA. Immel. 1986.

Rice, M. DILMUN DISCOVERED. Longman 1984.

Sanlaville, Paul and R. Paskoff. Shoreline changes in Bahrain since the beginning of human occupation. Bahrain Through the Ages. pp15-25. 1986.

Smith, G. Shallow-water reef fishes of Bahrain, personal communication from Dr. Greg Smith, University College of Bahrain.

Whelan, J. BAHRAIN, A MEED PRACTICAL GUIDE. MEED 1983.

Wray, et al. Commercial Fishes of Saudi Arabia. Min. of Ag. & Water, Saudi Arabia. 1979.

INDEX